Cricket Heroes

Essays by Members of the Cricket Writers Club

CRICKET HEROES

General Editor: David Lemmon

Queen Anne Press

A Queen Anne Press BOOK

First published in Great Britain in 1984 by
Queen Anne Press, a division of
Macdonald & Co (Publishers) Ltd,
Maxwell House, 74 Worship Street,
London EC2A 2EN

A BPCC plc Company

All photographs supplied by S & G Press Agency
Ltd except the following:
Page 133: *George Herringshaw (Associated Sports
Photography)*
Page 120: *Ken Kelly*
Pages 10, 19 and 30: *Marylebone Cricket Club*
Pages 127, 138 and 146: *Adrian Murrell (All-Sport)*

British Library Cataloguing in Publication Data
Cricket Heroes.
1. Cricket players — Biography
I. Lemmon, David
796.35'8'0922   GV915.A1

ISBN 0-356-10452-4

Typeset by SIOS Limited, London NW6

Printed and bound in Great Britain by
Hazell, Watson & Viney Limited
Member of the BPCC Group
Aylesbury, Bucks.

Contents

Introduction

THE CRICKET WRITERS CLUB

During the MCC's first post-war tour, to Australia in 1946-47, English and Australian journalists and broadcasters who were covering the tour set up an organisation called the Empire Cricket Writers Club. The aim of the club was to help members in their professional work and to field teams that played cricket throughout Australia, against schools and in charity matches. It was from this organisation that the Cricket Writers Club evolved, being officially founded at a meeting held in Nottingham during the first Test match between England and South Africa in 1947. The initial objective of the Cricket Writers Club was the promotion of cricket and cricket writing. After the inaugural meeting the club developed rapidly. It has never sought professional status in journalism but, negotiating on behalf of all cricket writers, it has been responsible for closer liaison with cricket administrators at home and overseas and for a wider understanding of the service cricket writing can render the first-class game.

The Cricket Writers Club won immediate esteem when, in the spring of 1948, it initiated a tradition of entertaining the visiting Australian team to dinner in London. The first Cricket Writers Club dinner was a memorable occasion. E. W. Swanton presided over the gathering, which numbered the Duke of Edinburgh among the guests, and the speeches, particularly those by Sir Donald Bradman, R. C. Robertson-Glasgow and Sir Norman Birkett, were so witty and entertaining that the BBC, who were broadcasting the function, extended their coverage and delayed the news. The dinner cost much more than was expected and although the club became solvent again as a result of donations by members, the ever-rising costs of organising such a function have meant the abandonment of the annual spring dinner in recent years. However, there are hopes that this custom of welcoming the tourists will be resurrected in the near future.

One tradition that has survived is the award to the 'Young Cricketer of the Year'. Each year members of the Cricket Writers Club select the player they consider most worthy of the award from among those who have had less than three years experience of first-class cricket. The award was first made in 1950 and among the winners since then have been Peter May, Colin Cowdrey, Freddie Trueman and, more recently, Norman Cowans. Membership of the Cricket Writers Club is by invitation and at present the membership is approximately 140, including leading cricket photographers like Ken Kelly and Patrick Eagar and leading statisticians like Wendy Wimbush and Bill Frindall.

In 1958 the Cricket Writers Club compiled its first book of *Cricket Heroes*. The book, published by Phoenix House, was a great success and now, more than a quarter of a century later, the club makes a second offering. The 20 members of the club who have contributed to this book were given complete freedom of choice, so readers may find some surprise omissions and some equally surprising inclusions. But then, a hero is an essentially personal choice. As the late Ian Peebles wrote in the first collection of *Cricket Heroes:* 'Every man should have his heroes. He is a poor character which cannot rejoice in the success of his fellow creatures and set the object of his admiration on a pedestal. The object of such adulation must, of course, vary enormously with the tastes and standards of the adulator and, indeed, the very man who shines in the eyes of one may be poison and anathema to another, although this, in the world of cricket with which we are concerned is unlikely.'

There is variety in this selection and, indeed, among the members of the Cricket Writers Club, but there is a consistency too, a consistency of tolerance, companionship and a love of the game.

C. T. Studd

ALAN GIBSON

Eton College in 1875 was not a place where one would expect an American evangelist of the kind called 'hot-gospelling' to go down well, especially if he was the only living man (so his English followers would sometimes affectionately aver) who pronounced 'Jerusalem' in two syllables. However, on 12 June that year, Quintin Hogg and John Graham, MP, armed with an introduction from Gladstone, called on the Provost. Several of the senior boys had expressed a desire to hear Dwight L. Moody, with his equally famous singer Ira D. Sankey, who were on a mission to Britain at the time. Graham and Hogg, both Old Etonians, wished to put up a tent in South Meadow, private land near the College, for a service on 22 June, boys to be admitted by free ticket. The Provost said he would not oppose the plan (though he later recanted). The Head Master said that in the event of Moody and Sankey 'coming to preach once in our neighbourhood I should not feel bound to put any special restriction upon our boys on the day selected'.

A few days later, Edward Knatchbull-Hugessen, MP, a vigorous High Churchman who had once risen to the heights of Under-Secretary of State for the Colonies, stormily descended upon Eton. He saw the tent with his own eyes, and was aghast that a 'Revival Meeting' was to be held there, and that Eton boys would be subjected to the 'semi-dramatic performances which have lately caused so much excitement in London'. He took the direst sanctions available to him, that is to say he wrote to *The Times* and *The Morning Post*. Seventy-four MPs, all Old Etonians or parents, added their names to the protest. The Marquess of Bath raised the matter in the House of Lords: 'Nothing', he declared, 'can be more calculated to interfere with good regulation in the management of the boys'.

Moody and Sankey nevertheless took the train to Windsor on the appointed day. Sankey, conscious of the importance of the

C. T. Studd (centre)

occasion, put on his best tie. Buckinghamshire police said they would not be responsible for order in the tent, so Graham and Hogg switched the meeting, with the Mayor of Windsor's consent, to Windsor Town Hall. Advised by the Superintendent of Police that 'the Eton boys have purchased a large quantity of eggs! There will be a breach of the peace!' the Mayor withdrew his permission, keeping well away from the site. However, the weather was fine, and a linen draper offered his large garden opposite. There were some 150 boys present, and several hundred adults – Old Etonians, masters, parents and townsfolk. There were four members of the Studd family: Edward, a wealthy businessman and a popular figure on the Turf, who had already heard and been converted by Moody, and his three sons, Kynaston, George and Charles, who were pupils. 'These four', wrote John Pollock many years afterwards, 'were to be the link between Moody's work for a nation, and his work for a world.'

The Studds were originally a Leicestershire family. According to Basil Cottle, the name 'Studd' may suggest associations with horse racing, which seems likely enough in Leicestershire. Father Edward decided to move, however, to Tedworth (now more commonly Tidworth) on the border between Wiltshire and Hampshire. He was a famous huntsman and MFH, and his sons were riding in little red jackets from the age of five or thereabouts. In his grounds at Tedworth Hall he laid out a racecourse. In 1866, one of his horses, Salamander, won the Grand National. Kynaston, George and Charles, as well as being trained horsemen, were all good cricketers, and were all in the Eton XI together. In due course they went on to Cambridge, and all became Cambridge captains, though not in chronological order: George was first in 1882, Charles in 1883, and Kynaston, who had gone up later than the others, in 1884. They soon became known simply by their initials: G. B., C. T. and J. E. K.

Because his career was so brief, it is not now remembered what a very good cricketer C. T. was. In 1882 he scored more than 1,000 runs and took more than 100 wickets. The only man to have done this before was the champion, W. G. Grace. Charles Studd did it again in 1883, his last season. All in first-class cricket, he scored 4,391 runs, average 30.49, and took 455 wickets, average 17. He played in five Tests, averaging 20. In the books, you will find his

career listed as lasting from 1879 to 1903, but that is because of a
few scattered matches he played for Middlesex when on furlough
from the missionary field. He bowled at medium pace, from a
considerable height, and broke from the off. His driving was the
principal feature of his batting, his accuracy of his bowling. H. S.
Altham says that he 'had at this time no superior amongst
amateurs as an all-round player'. This was a strange remark for
Altham to make, for although Studd *was* ahead of Grace in the
averages (not by much) those two seasons, you could hardly have
called him a 'superior player'. I have sometimes wondered if
Altham made a Freudian slip, and had unexpected doubts as to
how truly W. G. could be called an amateur.

The most famous match in which C. T. played was undoub-
tedly the Oval Test in 1882, though his own part of it was limited
and unhappy. There was only one Test, played at the end of
August. The Australians had lost four matches that year, two of
them against Cambridge sides – the University itself, and Cambridge Past and Present. One Australian is reported to have said,
ruefully, 'Show us a light blue cap and we'll run'. C. T. had scored
two centuries against them, and was an automatic choice for the
Test. This proved to be Australia's first victory in England. They
scored 63 and 122, England 101 and 77: Australia won by seven
runs. In England's first innings, Studd went in at number six and
was bowled by Spofforth for 0. Spofforth won the match for
Australia, taking 14 for 90 and bowling more than half their overs.
Studd's bowling was confined to four overs, 0 for 9, in the
Australian second innings. When England went in a second time,
needing 85, Hornby, the captain, held Studd back in the order,
saying he was keeping him in reserve for a crisis.

This was not a well-judged decision. After England had reached
51 for 2, the crisis developed with startling suddenness. Studd
became increasingly nervous, and according to C. I. Thornton,
not perhaps the most reliable of witnesses, was 'walking round the
pavilion with a blanket round him'. He did not go in until number
ten, and as it happened, did not receive a ball. Barnes and Peate,
batting at the other end, were both out before he had a chance.
Peate was out to a wild swish for which his explanation was that 'I
couldn't trust Maister Studd'. Much later, C. T., as if he had
heard the story about the blanket, said that 'the weather was cold.

We sat in the Committee Room, and the windows were shut because of the cold. Except that such strange things happen in cricket, none dreamed we should be beaten'. But Studd was a highly-strung man, and Peate's comment (though probably intended, and certainly regarded, as a wry joke from a non-batting Yorkshire slow left-arm bowler) may have had a touch of truth in it. It does seem, peering through the mists of time, that Hornby should have sent Studd in earlier.

I suppose the second most famous match in which Charles Studd took part – at least at the time, though forgotten now – was when, at the end of May that same year, Cambridge University had beaten the Australians. All three Studds took part. J. E. K. made 6 and 66, G. B. 42 and 48, and C. T. 117 and 17 not out. C. T. also took eight wickets and Cambridge won comfortably by six wickets. In the 'Varsity match that year, C. T. took nine wickets and made 69 in the second innings after G. B. had scored a century in the first. Oxford were beaten by seven wickets. There was a Studd in the Cambridge side every year from 1879 to 1884, and Cambridge won four of the six 'Varsity matches.

There was a plan to take an all-Cambridge side to Australia in the winter of 1882-83, under Hon. Ivo Bligh. This had to be modified – a couple of hardy Yorkshire professionals, Ulyett and Emmett, were recruited – but there was still a strong Cambridge representation. This was the side which regained 'the Ashes', or instituted 'the Ashes', or failed to regain them – the details are matters of complicated dispute to this day, and I am not going into them now. Both C. T. and G. B. joined the party. G. B.'s Test scores were 7, 0, 1, 3, 8 and 9. He did not bowl, though he took eight catches. That was the beginning and end of G. B.'s Test career, though we must remember that he was a sick man at the time, and had taken the trip partly for the sake of his health. In a career lasting from 1879 to 1886, he scored 2,892 runs, average 21.91, with three centuries. C. T. had a rather better tour. His Test scores were 0, 21, 14, 21, 25, 48 and 31, and he took three wickets. J. E. K., who became the first Studd baronet (P.M., a lineal successor, captained Cambridge in 1939) never played for England, but had his successes for Middlesex and became President of MCC in 1930. He had been Lord Mayor of London in 1929.

Looking back to the Oval Test of 1882, C. T.'s nervousness seems uncharacteristic of a man who was later to display unflinching courage, in far more trying circumstances, as a pioneering missionary in China, Africa and India. (There is an interesting contrast with W. G. Grace, who was never worried by any cricketing crisis, but at the end of his life was badly upset by the Zeppelins). His own explanation would have been, I expect, that in 1882, though he, Charles Studd, was a clean-living and devout man, and under the influence of Moody, he was not 'converted'. That experience came a little later, after he had watched by the bedside through a serious illness of brother George. By 1883 he felt he 'must go into the cricket field and get the men there to know the Lord Jesus'. He added 'My heart was no longer in the game. I wanted to win souls for the Lord'. The last sentences jar a little. Wanting to win souls for the Lord in no way required that he should not put his heart into cricket, as, for instance, in a later generation, T. C. Dodds and David Sheppard could have told him. But he did have a Christian influence on a number of leading cricketers, including the great A. G. Steel. Steel, and the Studds, often played cricket with Moody. Moody was amply built, but enthusiastic and surprisingly nimble, though he was more familiar with rounders.

In 1882 Moody and Sankey went on a mission to Cambridge. Kynaston had been partly responsible for the invitation and arrangements. There was mockery. Moody chose, bravely, to preach on Daniel in the den of lions. Of course he described himself as 'Dan'l'. The audience seized on it, and began to call out 'Dan'l! Dan'l!' whenever he paused. But he was good at not pausing, and had most of them on his side by the end of the meeting. It was to prove, in the following weeks, a triumphant visit. As one result, ultimately, a group was formed who became widely known as the Cambridge Seven. They dedicated themselves to the mission field, and included C. T. and Stanley Smith, who had stroked the University boat. They offered their services to the China Inland Mission. Very few people in England had heard of the China Inland Mission, but everyone had heard of Cambridge, if only because of the Boat Race, and the thought of seven young men, all distinguished in various ways, choosing to go from the latter to the former, caused a stir. After a preliminary series of meetings around the country to spread the Word, they left for China in February, 1885.

George was not one of the Cambridge Seven, but he was later to join Charles in missionary work. He went to the East, supposedly on a health trip to Japan, calling at Shanghai, where Charles was stationed. Charles wrote of George's visit: 'He had been converted some ten years before but had grown cold. He slept in my room at the Mission. I made a point of not speaking to him about religious things. The day after his arrival he booked his passage to Japan by a boat leaving a week afterwards, but he never sailed by it. The first few days he was much up at the Club playing cricket on their ground, and made a large score which advertised things a bit, for, of course, I went to see him play, and of course people wanted to know how this brother of his had "gone mad".' (Charles had been conducting some revival services in a lively, Salvation Army-type style, which had perturbed the English community, though the Chinese seemed to like them). 'My brother showed them very efficiently by "going mad" himself before the whole of Shanghai, and getting up a public meeting and telling them all about it. The consequence was that instead of going to Japan, he came into the interior of China with me. "If you, Charles", he afterwards said to me, "had tackled me on religion when we were rooming together, I should have sailed in that boat to Japan." The leadings of God are often mysterious but always perfect.'

However that may be, the incident shows a perceptive tact in Charles which many evangelists have lacked, and George's innings on the Shanghai ground deserves its niche in the history of cricket, for he spent many years as a missionary, ultimately moving to Los Angeles and becoming minister of a thriving, though down-town church. Kynaston also put in long spells working with Moody in the United States, helping with the organisation of the missions and developing the overseas contacts. He was the shrewdest of the brothers in practical matters, as his financial career indicated. None of them had any personal financial worries, because their father had left them in plenty, but they lived sparely, and contributed generously to the causes they had at heart.

I will not attempt to describe here Charles Studd's missionary career, but it is worth observing that his happiest and most successful years were in its last phase, in Central Africa. 'Bwana',

as he became known, died there on duty, as Livingstone had done
before him. Norman P. Grubb wrote a life of him, *C. T. Studd:
Cricketer and Pioneer*, which is worth reading, though marred by the
heavy hagiographical style common to the earlier publications of the
Religious Tract Society. We could do with a new one, more balanced, less reluctant to make criticisms. Geoffrey Moorhouse, with
his considerable knowledge of both cricket and foreign missions,
would be the man to do it.

Nor am I qualified to discuss the religious motivations of such a
family as the Studds, though I can understand some of them, for I
was brought up a Baptist (still am, come to that) and taught to revere
missionaries as members of an heroic profession. I think it is fair to
say that, like many evangelicals, C. T. was not a deep thinker. When
he left Eton, his housemaster wrote of him, 'Perhaps he might have
done more in work, but it is hard for the captain of the Eleven, and he
has done no little good to all who have come under his influence. I
think the secret of the charm of his character is that he thinks for
others rather than for himself'.

C. T.'s own comment on this was that he had learned more from
cricket than books, and this, when you come to think of it, is a
compliment to the game, or at least to the way it was played in those
days. Theologically, he saw things simply, in terms of black and
white. He preached to unsophisticated people, a task for which his
qualities of passionate sincerity, physical courage, and sheer loving
goodness equipped him superbly. He won hearts, or souls, he would
have preferred to say, by example more than anything else. He was
not one of the much-mocked missionaries who were said to convert
the natives by persuading them to put on trousers. When the Cambridge Seven went to China, they dressed in Chinese clothes, following the example of Hudson Taylor, who had founded the mission in
1865.

I doubt if Charles Studd would have been a success as a parson
of a fashionable Anglican West End church, had such an enter-
prise ever attracted him, in the 1880s; though I think he might
have been happy in the company of the Oxford Group, as Moral
Re-Armament was then known, in the 1930s. Peter Howard –also
an international athlete –was a man who would have appealed to
him. Or he could have made a name for himself as an itinerant
preacher for Wesley in the 1750s –remember Methodism also

sprang from Oxford. It is strange how strongly the spirit of revival continues to arise from time to time in our senior universities, which though no doubt palaces of light and learning, have customarily been austere, not to say toffee-nosed, in religious matters. Green's *Religion at Oxford and Cambridge, 1160-1960* is illuminating on the subject, though it still leaves us perplexed occasionally. He tells us how Studd and Smith prayed for a third friend, Beauchamp, 'every night after hall'. Beauchamp was soon arranging a weekly Bible reading for members of the First Trinity Boat Club, and joined the Cambridge Seven. And there was Paget Wilson, who was so inspired by the Oxford Christian Union that he spent the rest of his life in Japan where he succeeded in founding the Japan Evangelistic Band. Was it a brass band? What did they play? 'Climbing Up the Golden Stairs'? 'Sweeping Through the Gates'? 'From the Eastern Mountains'? (written by Thring who was a Balliol man and headmaster of Uppingham at about the same period. It was all very extraordinary, and I doubt if any of the University outbreaks of fervour have had more impact, nationally and internationally, than that of which the inspiration was Moody and the symbol the Cambridge Seven.

This is the best judgement I can make of Charles Studd: I will venture to say that of all the men in this book, he – in more than a cricketing sense – came nearest to heroism. No, perhaps not 'heroism'. It is an awkward word, with too many meanings, and can be used too cheaply. Let us instead settle for 'sainthood'.

Maurice Tate

JOHN ARLOTT

Mention the name of Maurice Tate to any pre-1940 cricketer and his first reaction will be a nostalgic smile, for 'Chub' was a happy, convivial companion. He was, too, beyond doubt one of the greatest of all bowlers. He played for Sussex and England; technically he was a unique, attacking fast-medium bowler; a great-hearted trier, most generous of cricketers, magnificently – if sometimes unconsciously – humorous; loyal, and a warm family man. It is not possible to demonstrate, nor to measure, Maurice Tate's greatest gift, that of immense speed off the pitch. It used to be said by those who batted against him that his bowling actually gained pace as it bounced. That senior wrangler of cricket, Bob Wyatt, argued that only a positive top-spinner could do that. All others, he maintained, were bound to lose pace in overcoming the drag of the ground. Having made that point, he was completely content to state that, in his experience, Maurice Tate lost less pace off the pitch than any other bowler of his kind.

Statistically, although an unusually late starter for a pace bowler – 29 years old when he came to his first Test – who played only 39 times for England, he took 155 wickets at 26.16. Moreover, he achieved his success with, surely, less support than any other major English bowler ever enjoyed – suffered, probably, is the better word. It should be stressed, too, that he played in years – 1924 to 1932 – when wicket preparation, especially in Australia, was so loaded in favour of the batsmen that the laws were changed to give bowlers even a remotely fair chance: too late, though, for Maurice Tate. Had the new lbw law of 1937-72 applied in his day, he might well have taken several hundred more wickets, and great batsmen would not – in the contempt of legislated safety – have played his ferocious breakback with their pads. He was one of the few people who could, and did, grin, if ruefully, when that happened. This was but one facet of the generally-

Maurice Tate

recognised fact that he was a most unlucky bowler, in terms, not
only of 'beating everything' without taking a wicket, but also
often, because of his fierce bounce, of dropped catches. This he
accepted, if not with a grin, with an oath, no grudges and renewed
effort.

The career of Maurice Tate was shaped by four events over
which he had little influence. He was not even present at the first.
In 1902 the Australians came to England. The first two Test
matches were drawn; Australia won the third. The summer was
wet, with pitches much to the liking of Fred Tate, a somewhat
portly slow-medium off-spinner of Sussex, who accordingly
enjoyed his best season. As a result, on 24 July, 1902 – which was
his 35th birthday – he walked out at Old Trafford to play for
England for the first time, in, as it proved, one of the epic Tests of
cricket history. Not to dwell on the other aspects of a splendid
game, when Australia batted a second time 37 ahead, Lockwood,
at his most savage, took their first three wickets for ten runs. At
16, Joe Darling, the Australian captain, and a left-hander, hit Len
Braund with the leg-spin and Fred Tate, running first the wrong
way to what Braund called 'a boomerang of a ball' dropped the
catch. Darling (37) and Gregory put on another 48 before Tate (2
for 7) and Lockwood ended the innings for 86.

Next day, after a morning downpour, England – needing 124 to
win – reached 92 for 3 before Trumble and Saunders cut into the
batting. When Lilley was caught they had reached 116 for 9 –
eight wanted – but as Tate, last man, walked out, rain began
again. He could not come to the crease for threequarters of an
hour. Then he edged his first ball for four, but the next bowled
him. England had lost the match – and the rubber with it – by
three runs. Fred Tate had failed at the last; but, if he had caught
Darling, the situation presumably would never have arisen.

He and Len Braund were to travel down to London together.
As they sat in the dressing-room, Fred Tate said 'I lost the match'
and a tear ran down his cheek. Braund countered with one of the
great comments of sporting history: 'Go on, Fred, get upstairs and
get your money – it's only a game'. Fred Tate was not comforted.
Not even Len Braund's bubbling humour could lift him out of his
depression. Once during their train journey he suddenly stiffened
and said 'I've a little kid at home who'll make it up for me'.

That season Fred Tate took 180 wickets at 15.71, and played for England. Within three years he had left county cricket; walked out of his pub at Haywards Heath; left his native Sussex to coach, restlessly, at Oundle School, Gillingham and Plumstead. He did not want to play cricket, even though 20 years afterwards when he was coach at Trent College, he still looked a first-class spin bowler in the nets. Fred Tate had been called 'lucky' when he was picked to play for England at Old Trafford; in the outcome it virtually broke his heart. His son – seven years old in 1902 – could not remember that ever, after that, his father talked of cricket, coached or advised him. Maurice was keen but, in his own words, a less than average boy cricketer. There was probably a considerable element of sympathy in the Sussex club's offer to the leggy 15-year-old of a trial and, subsequently, a job on the ground staff at a pound a week – for the season only, of course.

Maurice tried and worked and worked and tried and, in fact, he loved life 'on the staff'. With the copying idolatry of the child, he bowled exactly like his father; and batted a bit. When war broke out in 1914 he was 20, had been on the staff for five years and the height of his potential seemed to be a somewhat less talented county cricketer than his father. Loyal and keen as he was, he had hardly made a mark on the game. In 13 county matches he had scored 153 runs and taken 22 wickets.

When he came back from army service he had filled out, was fit and strong and wanted to earn a married man's wage. Sussex were doubtful. Indeed it was not until they discovered that six main players would not be back from the war in time for the 1919 – two-day match – season; that since their two key bowlers were in their mid-40s, they signed him on. He had four years to make up, and his development in 1919 was slow; but 1920 was his first thousand-run season, and he took 50 wickets. In the next two seasons he worked his way up the batting order; and a second-wicket stand of 385 with Ted Bowley in 1921 helped to establish him. He bowled regularly, but without his father's subtlety of flight, pushing his off-breaks through at a pace near medium.

At the end of July, 1922, in the Eastbourne week, the second formative event of his life took place. After Hampshire lost two wickets cheaply, that all but impregnable left-hander Philip Mead settled in at his most obdurate. Maurice Tate was wheeling away his accurate, but not particularly penetrative, off-spinners, when suddenly, for no reason he could afterwards recall, he decided to 'let him have one'. From his usual approach, he put full effort into a ball which pitched off stump, fired off the pitch and hit the top of the leg with Mead's stroke only half complete. Tate was both surprised and delighted. Arthur Gilligan, his captain, standing at mid-off, stiffened, startled. Mead walked out, imperturbable as ever. Questioned about that ball 30 years later, he remembered it distinctly. 'First fast ball, and the best I've ever seen him bowl', he said. Had he made any comment to him? 'Not me, I never encouraged bowlers.'

It was as near to a cricketing miracle as the history of the game contains. Suddenly the sharpest attacking weapon of his time had been thrust into the hand of an industrious but rather pedestrian county all-rounder. Crucially, he had the strength and stamina to employ it. Arthur Gilligan, sensing an immense asset of strength to Sussex, was almost equally excited. Tate finished that Hampshire innings with 4 for 69 and took 1 for 10 in the second. In the next match, against Essex, he took four of their first five wickets. The new power, though, was heady; in the second innings he could not control his line of swing, but of his new-found pace from the pitch there was no doubt.

The metamophorsis of 'young Chub' went round the cricket world like a bush fire. While the Sussex club buzzed with the news of its splendid new asset, there was serious discussion. The decision was for the moment, at least, to do nothing, lest through interference, the gift disappeared as inexplicably as it had appeared. His most effective ball was a sharp body-action break-back which burst through some famous defences. It was considered impolitic to attempt to add more at that time.

Meanwhile Tate had not, at first – and who could have expected or asked as much – full control or exploitation of its possibilities. What he had was impressive. At first he rarely had outstanding figures in both innings; but those for one were impressive enough. On the Bank Holiday on an easy Hove pitch, Middlesex were reduced to 26 for 5, and Tate finished the innings with 6 for 30. Against Leicestershire, 4 for 83; Lancashire, 5 for 61; Worcestershire, 4 for 46; Northamptonshire, 5 for 19; and finally, Yorkshire, the County Champions, were put out for 42, 5 for 20.

The spring nets of 1923 could not come quickly enough for Maurice Tate. Working with Arthur Gilligan, who bowled it naturally, he set out to develop the out-swinger; to the delight of Sussex it came almost at once. At first he went cautiously, striving for accuracy. In the first match, against Essex, he took 5 for 93 and scored 170 runs; at Cambridge, 51 runs, 5 wickets for 60; against Northamptonshire, at Hove, 5 for 72. There were times – they continued throughout his career – when he did too much; beat the bat of men not good enough to edge him, and the stumps as well. Middlesex, the Whitsun match at Lord's, on a batsman's wicket, saw 7 for 114. Then to the batsmen's land of plenty at The Oval; a major sustained bowling operation, seven wickets – all in the top half of the order – for 122 in the match.

The breakthrough had to come. At Hove, Essex bowled out Sussex for 100, then Tate took a monumentally steady 4 for 20 in 30 overs. Essex went in at the end of the second afternoon needing 236 to win. Maurice Tate bowled down their first four wickets for five runs that night. Next morning he took four more: 8 for 37 in the innings; 12 for 57 in the match. Such figures were all he needed to establish his confidence. Now he became all but irresistible. He finished the season with 219 wickets – more than anyone else in the country – at the remarkable average of 13.97, and, for more than good measure, scored 1,168 runs.

The third of his formative influences was his bowling partnership with Arthur Gilligan, described by *Wisden* as 'about the best fast bowler in the country'. Constantly they took seven or eight wickets between them in an innings. In 1923, in the win over Nottinghamshire (second in the Championship) at Horsham, Tate took 13 for 68 runs, Gilligan 7 for 66. They were both included in *Wisden*'s 'Five Bowlers of the Year' which said of Tate 'In 1922 he found his true *métier*, and last summer he was by general consent the best bowler in England. Though much slower than Gilligan through the air, he often comes off the ground quite as fast'.

His outstanding individual performance was in the Test trial at Lord's. The Rest were 200 for 4 at lunch; in a quarter of an hour afterwards, Maurice Tate took the wickets of Carr, Chapman, Geary, Macaulay and Louden – four bowled and one lbw – without a run scored from him. If there had been Test matches that summer, he must have been a first bowling choice for England. He and his friends, and the aging Fred Tate up in the Midlands, looked forward to the season of 1924.

Those with the fortune to have watched Maurice Tate in his great years retain a memory of grace, if not absolute beauty, in a bowling action. He was not obviously physically prepossessing; his shoulders were strong, but sloping; chest deep, arms fairly long; hips wide – ideal to cushion the shock of the delivery stamp – and his feet, to the pleasure of the cartoonists, a hearty, wide 12. He never used more than the eight-yard run he, and his father before him, employed for slow-medium off-breaks. Two short walking steps; then eight smoothly accelerating strides and a controlled leap. Then, as he rocked back on the right foot, body absolutely sideways on to the batsman, the camera might catch a clear diagonal across the body, from the fingers of the high-pointing left hand down to the right, cupping the ball. In the final splendour of delivery, as the right arm swung over at full height to the release, the straight left leg plunged to the ground and the whole body swung forward, sometimes so fully that the knuckles of his right hand scraped the ground. Perhaps the keynote was that prodigal stamp of the left foot which seemed to jolt, but not to inhibit, his entire body swing. George Cox junior used to say that, especially when the earth was damp, he – or anyone else at cover point – felt the ground shake at the impact. Many bowlers follow through violently; but not to such an extent. In Maurice Tate that was as unusual as his amazing pace off the pitch; and it is difficult not to link the two as cause and effect.

To his natural breakback he had added out-swing; and, according to his captains, when he tired, he had a sharp in-swinger. He delivered, too, with the seam so straight – with, or against the swing, or from straight – as to move sharply off the pitch. Then he was often at his most effective. He could command swing but not seam movement. Once he bowled Frank Woolley with a ball which dipped in, moved back and hit the off stump. 'Chub,' said the batsman, 'you meant that to go the other way.' 'Let me tell you, Stork,' Maurice replied, 'I haven't got the vaguest bloody idea where it's going, so I'm damned sure you haven't'. When batsmen saw the black mark where Maurice Tate pitched on a green top they resolved to play forward, straight, carefully and hopefully. Such was that speed of bounce that it was a maxim of the time never to play back at Maurice Tate with the new ball. Frank Lee used to relate how as a new batsman with Somerset he was told by Tom Young: 'Don't dare play back to Chubby until you've been in an hour'. After about half an hour with 15 or so runs on the board he moved back to glance him and saw his leg stump plucked out before he was halfway through his stroke.

This was the bowler, mature in cricketing knowledge but young in his fresh gift, who went into the season of 1924. Sussex surprised even their best friends. Rain shortened many matches, but Tate and Gilligan between them put out Cambridge for 121 and 158; Hampshire 129; Gloucestershire 79; Worcestershire 89; Essex 137 and 152; Somerset 161 and 101; Surrey (who finished third) 53; Middlesex (runners-up) 104 and 41. So to the first Test against South Africa at Edgbaston. Gilligan was appointed captain of England and Tate was capped for the first time. Herby Taylor, winning the toss, put England in. Hobbs and Sutcliffe, opening for the first time, put on 136 in an England total of 438. When South Africa batted, Gilligan, taking the first over, bowled Catterall, and threw the ball to Tate to take the other end. His first ball in Test cricket was a breakback, and too fast for Susskind, who nicked it to Kilner at short leg. The Sussex pair bowled unchanged; Gilligan 6 for 7, Tate 4 for 12; to put South Africa out for 30 in an hour and a quarter. The pitch rolled out slower, but Gilligan, 5 for 83, and Tate, 4 for 103, gave England an innings win; the 20th South African wicket fell to a run out. Life, though, was to change for them both within days.

They went straight to Horsham and the Sussex match with Worcestershire. There Gilligan, with figures of 4 for 64 and 2 for 37, and Tate, 4 for 96 and a quite explosive 8 for 18, routed Worcestershire in two days. Then on from Horsham to Lord's where, on a good batting wicket, they took nine wickets between them (for 229 runs) and South Africa were again beaten by an innings. Next to Gentlemen versus Players at The Oval where a ball from Dick Pearson of Worcestershire getting up freakishly off a length hit Arthur Gilligan over the heart. The bruising was extremely heavy: although he should have rested, he persisted in playing on and, in the second innings, scored a spectacular 112 in an attempt to save the match. The outcome was a cardiac condition which prevented him, on all but a few courageous occasions, from ever bowling truly fast again. He became a thoughtful practitioner at medium pace, but his injury meant that Maurice Tate had no effective bowling partner during his best years. After the Gilligan injury, Tate took 9 for 106 in the third Test which England won by nine wickets; and six in the rain-spoilt fourth and fifth.

This fourth influential event in his life, though, had committed him, for the remainder of his finest period, to the virtually impossible combination of shock-and-stock bowler for both country and county. Sussex wanted him also as a batsman. Fortunately for him and his captains, he was a strong, willing man, whose training had been based on length and line. Figures can be misleading, but they illustrate accurately the extent and success of Maurice Tate's efforts, especially over the 14-year period of his high plateau; 1922-35. (In 1933, most unusually for one all but immune to injury, he had to miss eight matches.) During that 14-year period, in 19 seasons or tours he averaged 1,201.4 overs and 135 wickets; or, more impressively, 1,630.5 overs and 184 wickets a year for 14 years.

By any standard, that is a most imposing list; 200 wickets and 1,000 runs in each of three seasons, five 'ordinary' doubles, plus one in India. In six seasons between 1923 and 1932 he took more wickets than anyone else in the country. His total figures from 1912 to 1937 – remembering that in the three pre-war years he played in only 15 matches, and then lost four seasons to the war – were:

Batting – Innings 970; Runs 21,717; Highest score 203; Not outs 102; Average 25.01;Centuries 27; 10 times 1,000 runs, including one tour of India.

Bowling – Wickets 2,784; Runs 21,717; Average 18.16; 14 times 100 wickets in a season, including one tour of India.

Only eight other men have achieved over 20,000 runs and 2,000 wickets. His large proportion of maidens means not only that he was steady but also reflects the fact that he left many batsmen groping, unable to get a touch; and drove others on to the defensive or simply 'struck them on the bat'.

Then, to put flesh on the bones of the figures, to Australia under Arthur Gilligan in a team with virtually no bowling to support him. It had been said that his type of bowler never succeeded in Australia and at first he hesitated about bowling with his full follow-through on to the left foot. Once he discovered that he needed to bowl a yard shorter, though, he became extremely menacing, even on those rock-like pitches. No Australian batsman played him with certainty. Collins tried to 'farm' him: to an extent he succeeded, but Tate took his wicket six times in ten. In Adelaide, when he tore the nail from his left big toe, he cut a slit in his boot and bowled on. Within three weeks, still in immense pain and wearing a special boot, he took seven wickets in the only Test of the series that England won. It was heroic; and it effectively smashed his left foot. In that series Maurice Tate bowled 316 eight-ball overs – more than any other two English players; and took as many wickets, 38 – a new record for an England-Australia series – as any three of them put together; and for a quarter of the runs scored.

So by the end of the Australian tour after only nine months of international cricket he had taken 65 Test wickets. He was still to play the major part in England's two historic triumphs – in taking The Ashes from Australia in 1926, and beating them again in 1928-29 for the first time in Australia for 17 years. In that rubber he took 17 wickets; 12 of batsmen in the first six places; and only one lower than eighth. A leg injury kept him out of two South African Tests in 1929; but he still took ten wickets – more than anyone else except Freeman – and all were of major batsmen.

In 1930 it had been said that, at 35, he was too old to tackle the Australian batting. He began the first Test by taking the wickets of Ponsford, Woodfull and Bradman for eight runs; in all, six of their best wickets for 89. His 5 for 124 (in a total of 566) helped a draw at Leeds; rain spoiled the Old Trafford game and at The Oval he, too, was overwhelmed in the Australian 695. Nevertheless, he had taken 15 wickets – five more than any other English bowler – 13 of them in the top half of the order. He did, too, take their first six wickets for 18 when they came down to Hove.

Tate was top of the bowling averages for Tests and the tour of South Africa in 1930-31. He had no place in Douglas Jardine's plans for the 1932-33 series in Australia but, on form, he had to be

picked for the tour. Even when he did have a chance to bowl in a
worthwhile match – against New South Wales – he was not given
the new ball. Nevertheless, he picked off four of their first five
batsmen – Wendell Bill, Don Bradman, Alan Kippax and Stan
McCabe – for 53 before Jardine put him under wraps for New
Zealand. He was brought in for a single Test there and recalled for
one against South Africa in 1935, but effectively his England
career was over. Since for most of his career he shouldered the
pace attack almost alone, his record is most impressive:

Batting –   Innings 52; Not outs 5; Runs 1,198; Highest score
                 100 not out; Average 25.48.
Bowling –   Balls 12,523; Runs 4,055; Wickets 155; Average
                 26.26; Best bowling 6 for 42.

Against Australia, almost a lone hand on over-perfect wickets in a
day of batting records and often against Bradman, his figures
show the extent of his effort. He bowled 1,175 overs, more than a
quarter of them maidens (184 of them eight-ball maidens), and
took 83 wickets at 30 runs apiece.

   He had another five years of county cricket. He was still capable
of hostile spells, and still no-one in the country exploited a green
top more effectively. Thus he played a considerable part in the
best Championship run of Sussex history; when they were
runners-up for three consecutive seasons from 1932 to 1934.
Frequently he captained the side with considerable wisdom, and
characteristic humour and good nature; and he remained to the
end one of the most popular cricketers in the world. He made a
hospitable and popular publican – if not, because of his generos-
ity, a financially successful one – at Wadhurst and Robertsbridge.
He was bowling at the nets, in 1981, the day before he came home,
went upstairs feeling tired and dropped instantly dead from heart
failure. Always impatient of illness, even – perhaps especially –
his own; he would have been glad to go quickly. He will be
remembered as a cricketer with an unique gift of pace from the
pitch. As a man, a good husband, father and friend; he was missed
as greatly as he was loved.

Douglas Jardine

TONY PAWSON

Hero-worship is a schoolboy emotion, so even if a love of cricket keeps many of us perpetually young, our adulation of a cricketer can never again be as intense as in those early years. Appropriately, I was only 11 years old when my imagination was caught by a man who has always kept a special place in my mind – Douglas Robert Jardine.

A strange choice, some may think, when he is more often remembered as villain than hero; as the man who nearly lost a Dominion rather than the captain who won the Ashes. But what a victory that was – a 4-1 win in Australia with Don Bradman at the height of his power. Jardine's tactical innovation of leg theory, and the use of a battery of fast bowlers, was highly imaginative for his day, however commonplace it has since become. It was, too, the basis of the one victory in a long, arid period of abject English failure.

That was the basis of my early devotion to our Iron Duke of the cricket field. Nothing was so important in my young life as that we should win the Ashes. I had had to endure our crushing home defeat in 1930 at the hands of Australia and Bradman – or rather I should say Bradman and Australia to get the priorities right. There was an illusory win for England in the first Test at Nottingham. Even then the Don's second-innings century nearly turned it for Australia, before he failed to pick up Robins' googly (an inability to spot the googly appears to have been the only chink in Bradman's armour apart from the one Jardine exploited). But from that English victory devastating defeat was born. Robins used to relate that as the Don marched out past him, bitterly disappointed despite a brilliant century that would have satisfied most young players, he made a brief comment to the bowler. With Don's voice higher and squeakier than usual in the emotion of the moment Robins couldn't quite catch the words: 'I wasn't sure

Douglas Jardine

whether he said "Just wait for Lord's" or for "Leeds". It didn't much matter which it was. He made 254 at Lord's and 334 at Leeds'. So we lost the series 2-1, and in the next 22 years only Jardine won the Ashes for us.

What is more natural, therefore, than that he should be my hero. Add to that a special affinity because I was at his old preparatory school, Horris Hill near Newbury, where we were given a holiday in honour of his victory. That was enough to endear him to any schoolboy. Later I was to follow in the great man's footsteps in a minor way, captaining Winchester's cricket XI and playing for Oxford. There was also the continuing attraction of opposites. My own carefree approach to the game was in the 'amateur' tradition (though it was often professionals such as Denis Compton or Godfrey Evans who were the ultimate expression of it) while the 'amateur' Jardine was totally austere, dedicated and professional in his cricket. I always went out of my way to touch my cap to umpires and fast bowlers to keep them sweet. Jardine, like Trevor Bailey, was nerveless enough not to give a damn if he antagonised them, and was happy to face whatever they might hurl at him. For me cricket was always a game to enjoy – but essentially just a game. For Jardine it was a serious business.

In one thing only was I completely at one with him. Whatever your attitude to a game, if you play it at any level, you should play to win, with every fibre of your being devoted to doing well. There is no sympathy from me for the 'sporting loser' reputation in which so many Englishmen seem to take pride. A loser is just a loser. And having taken part in an Olympic Games I know what the competitors think about 'the taking part being more important than the winning'. Most of them class it as a bit of romantic nonsense or a feeble excuse for personal failure. In the Helsinki Games of 1952 we had to wait until the final round of the final event for a gold medal, and then it was a horse that won it for us, with Foxhunter getting a little help from Colonel Llewellyn. I didn't take much pleasure in Britain's overall performance, and I doubt if Jardine would have, either.

We have been treated to many rumours that a film on the 'Bodyline' series of 1932-33 is contemplated by David Puttnam as a follow-up to *Chariots of Fire*, with Jardine firmly cast as the demon king, and 'Gubby' Allen as the angel of light, who refused to bowl

the deadly and unsporting leg theory. If the film is ever produced,
which appears increasingly doubtful, it is hoped that the theme
will not be at variance with reality. But certainly these two protagonists' paths had crossed frequently from early youth. When at
Horris Hill Jardine was bowled for a 'duck' by Allen, who was
playing for Summerfields Preparatory School. Jardine had the
better of it when he captained Winchester to win at Eton in 1919,
with Allen not making the Eton team for that match, though he
was in the side most of the season as a batsman. Jardine had gone
on to Oxford when Allen was again a loser in 1920, despite taking 9
for 34 in Winchester's first innings. Allen retaliated triumphantly
the next year with his 5 for 20 and 4 for 74, winning Eton an
extraordinary match in which J.L. Guise made 278 out of Winchester's second innings total of 381.

At Oxford Jardine did not realise his full potential, being ham-
pered by an injury and an addiction to work, which was not a
disease from which all his undergraduate contemporaries suffered. In 1921 Oxford lost the 'Varsity match by an innings with a
negligible contribution from Jardine, who, however, scored two
centuries and averaged 46.25 for Oxford that season, scoring over
1,000 runs in the summer, when he also played for Surrey in the
long vacation. It was for Surrey that Jardine was playing when
Allen made the Cambridge team as a freshman in 1922, promptly
racing Oxford to an innings defeat after Percy Chapman had set up
the win with a not-out century. At a higher level, the rivalry
continued with Jardine making good with Surrey at The Oval,
leading the averages in 1927 with 91.00 per innings, and Allen
across London with Middlesex at Lord's. Even when they were
together in the England team they went their separate ways with
Allen threatening to return home if asked to bowl to a packed
leg-side field, which he regarded as unsporting. The fact that he
was prepared to jeopardise a Test place makes this a more likely
reason than the one advanced by Bill Bowes, another fast bowler
on the tour, who believes that Allen lacked the control at his
tearaway pace to bowl successfully to a particular field placing.
Whatever the reason, the fact is that Jardine was sensible enough
not to force the issue, and to make such good use of Allen that
'Gubby' made a major contribution to victory with 21 wickets at
28.23. So what was all the fuss about in that far-off, but never

forgotten, 'Bodyline' series, and what was Jardine's part? He was the natural choice as captain. On the previous tour to Australia Jardine had played a resolute part in the team's victory, his stand of 262 with Hammond in the fourth Test being instrumental in a 12-run win for England, and, less importantly, a record. In 1931 he had his first experience of captaincy in first-class cricket, leading England in the series against New Zealand, and in the following year he excelled in the only Test against India. He was the obvious selection as the man with the strength of will to win against the odds in Australia. Given that instruction, he applied his whole mind and being to the task. And he had the character to succeed.

Jardine had been a strong, determined, mature man even in his Winchester days. The keeper of the Wykehamist records, Gerry Dicker, played with him there and recalls: 'He was never young. He had a confidence and self-sufficiency beyond his years. As captain of Lords (the Winchester XI) he went his own way and argued down such eminent cricket masters as Harry Altham and Rockley Wilson'. Mark Patten, who kept wicket for Winchester and Oxford when Jardine was playing, was also a close acquaintance, and watched that famous tour. This is his view of Jardine: 'He was a typical Scot in his rather dour sense of humour, but I found him a delightful companion and a highly intelligent cricket captain. When he was put in charge of the tour he was determined not to emulate Percy Chapman, whom he regarded as having contributed to the previous defeat in England by his cavalier and flippant attitude. He had no respect either for one of his tour managers. "Plum" Warner had been a great cricketer in his day, but Jardine regarded him as a fussy old has-been, and any contribution from Warner was likely to be ignored, or taken as a reason for doing the exact opposite'.

The leg theory tactics had been worked out by Jardine primarily to counter Bradman's phenomenal run-scoring, but also because on the then plumb Australian pitches it was fatal to bowl to a split field. You had to pack one side or the other. While Australians claimed it was designed for intimidation, with its inner and outer circle of leg-side fielders and with the ball bowled at or wide of the leg-stump, the facts made it clear that was not the prime intent. The early overs, when the ball was hard and bouncy and intimida-

tion easiest, were bowled to off-side fields, since the shine then
gave hope of slip or wicket catches from the swing. It was taking
wickets, not injuring players, at which Jardine aimed his tactics
and his awesome weapon, Harold Larwood. How well he succeeded. But the tour was overwhelmed by a welter of controversy
once Australia began to lose. Once their captain, Bill Woodfull,
was struck over the heart and complained of England's lack of
sportsmanship, and the Australian Board of Control made a similar complaint in a cable to MCC. While there was a Test series to
win Jardine was given support by the cricket authorities; afterwards the main concern was mending bridges with Australia.
Larwood was fêted by mass crowds, but then asked to apologise to
Australia for the type of attack, which MCC had maintained was
perfectly fair. Being a man of character, like Jardine, Larwood
refused and his England career was ended by refusing that
ludicrous command.

Jardine's vice-captain, Bob Wyatt, another firm and thoughtful
cricketer, was in fact the first to exploit the leg theory tactics in an
early tour match, for which Jardine rested. He, like the rest of the
team whom Jardine consulted and from whom, with the exception
of Allen, he had full backing, accepted the tactics. The myths that
have been assiduously built to damn Jardine should have been laid
to rest by a recent balanced television documentary using film of
the time. This recalled that the only three cases of Australians
being severely struck – Woodfull twice, Oldfield once – were
when Larwood was bowling on or outside the off-stump to
orthodox off-side fields, and Oldfield at least was quick to declare
his injury was entirely his own fault. Once the shine was off, and
the ball soft, it was also clear that it came through not much above
stump height despite Larwood's pace. But the really revealing
comment on this massive storm in a teacup was from the
Australian, H.H. Alexander. When the series was already lost he
was brought in to bowl fast and retaliatory bouncers at Jardine and
co. As he said: 'I hit him on the knuckles. I hit him in the groin. I
hit him on the thigh. But he never flinched. He had a ton of guts' –
unlike some of our squealers was the implied addition.

That film must have confirmed for those who never saw 'Bodyline' in action how correct was Jardine in his foreword to the book,
Bodyline?, which Larwood wrote immediately after the tour: 'It is

curious to think that had you been playing for Australia you would have been the most popular man there! As it is I gather that you were not even permitted to depart unmolested and in peace. No bowler has ever had to contend with more than fell to your lot, or "stuck it" more magnificently – and by the same token no bowler can show a fairer, finer or more convincing record. More than half the 33 wickets you took in the Test matches were clean bowled, or its equivalent leg before wicket – 18 to be exact. This on the perfect, toned-down wickets of Australia, where numbers one to seven in the batting order are far less frequently clean bowled than in England. If this isn't bowling at the wicket I don't know what is. As M.A. Noble, the old Australian captain, wrote in summing up the tour: "It's all humbug to say his tactics were unfair or that he bowled at the man instead of the wicket. He didn't." Have you heard the sound of the film of the third Test match? I am told it is louder than a war film!'

That summed up the Australian reaction – all sound and fury signifying nothing except a dislike of losing. And for that my 'hero' was soon ditched and has had his name persistently blackened by biased and unbalanced criticism. Before he bowed out of the Test scene Jardine gave the perfect demonstration of how to play fast bouncers as he made 127 off the West Indian pace bowlers Constantine and Martindale, who were trying him out with his own medicine. He had indeed 'tons of guts', and a relentless determination. Once the captaincy was passed on to those less tactically aware, or less resolute, we were a long time winning again with Allen even contriving to lose after leading 2-0 in Australia.

In his book Larwood wrote: 'We of the England XI would have gone anywhere and done anything for our skipper. England will be fortunate indeed if it ever has to serve under a better man than Jardine'. That view Larwood confirmed in the recent television programme despite all the subsequent misrepresentation and unfair denegration of Jardine's name. The praise may be over-generous, but it reads truer than the persistent vilification based on bias. Larwood also posed this question to the barrackers in Australia: 'Would you have behaved in similar outrageous fashion to me had I been Tim Wall bowling for Australia?' It was a question that hardly needed an answer, but time has supplied one.

When Lillee and Thomson were bowling a far more lethal form of
Bodyline there was no outcry against it. Instead Australian bowlers and spectators delighted in drawing blood and there was
uproarious support typified by the chants: 'Ashes to ashes, dust to
dust – if Thomson don't get ya, Lillee must!'

It was not Jardine and Larwood, but Lillee and Thomson and
the West Indian fast bowlers bouncing the ball sometimes from
round the wicket who were the ones to force batsmen to wear
protective helmets and body padding. In 1932-33 it was only the
punsters who commented:

'Oh, they'd be a lot calmer
In Ned Kelly's armour
When Larwood the wrecker begins.'

In practice the leg theory on toned-down pitches with old-style
cricket balls which went soft after a few overs was a picnic compared to what has since been accepted without protest.

My only meeting with my hero did little to boost my confidence. Just before the war Jardine brought The Butterflies side to
play Winchester College in what was usually a happy-go-lucky
game. Mindful of past practice I wandered on to the field as
Winchester captain to tell Jardine that if he would take an early
tea, I would declare in half an hour. No one ever stopped a more
imperious rocket on the subject of messing about with previously
agreed times. But he quite approved when, instead, we batted on
and left the visitors a couple of hours to make an impossible total.
Larwood had written 'Mr Jardine is well able to take care of
himself. If I know him at all that which he says will be withering
and final'. I can echo that, only adding fair and sensible as well.

After listening to that impressive homily as I looked up in all
respects to that lofty figure with his jutting jaw and certainty of
right and wrong I am left with a fantasy of my own. In his book
Sort of a Cricket Person Jim Swanton deplores the effect of the
Evening Standard's tennis correspondent, Bruce Harris, being
sent to cover that controversial tour in his place because he had
missed his deadline when reporting on Holmes and Sutcliffe's
record 555 first wicket stand at Leyton. The *Standard* apparently
felt that if Jim couldn't get his story back from the East End, he
was even less likely to get it back from Melbourne or Sydney. Jim
however believes that if he had gone, he would have come down

heavily against Jardine and 'if I had done so, this must have made for a rather different climate of opinion in England'. Swanton trying to stop Jardine employing his favoured tactics is a fascinating thought. A battle between the two might have been a title fight between the two heavyweights when Swanton was at the height of his reputation. But as a young reporter of 25 on his first overseas tour? No contest, I think, but I would have liked to have witnessed it! It is symptomatic of the 'balanced' assessments of that tour that Jim's account doesn't even mention Harold Larwood's *Bodyline?* (a prime source, if ever there was one) among the relevant literature on which Jardine should be judged. Instead he picks on Fingleton's *Cricket Crisis* as the definitive 'objective' account. Larwood may be regarded as too subjective, too close to the experience, but so was Jack Fingleton; one of the most embittered failures in that Australian team.

Jardine and Larwood were supported until the series was won, then rapidly shunted into oblivion. When the Australians reverted to their winning ways in England in 1934 there was no Larwood, no Voce and no Jardine for them to face. Imagine that happening to Ian Chappell, Lillee, Thomson and co! How right that great Surrey and England cricketer, Percy Fender, was to call the treatment of Jardine and Larwood 'a climb-down' and add 'it was a tragedy in sport as great as I have ever known. I don't think the Australians would have been so conciliatory if things had been the other way round'. He can say that again, as we now well know.

We were back to being good fellows and good losers. But I still light a candle to the memory of the man who was resolute enough and able enough to defeat the Australians and briefly brighten my youth.

Denis Compton

JOHN THICKNESSE

Cricket-mad schoolboys in the years after the war had a straight-forward choice of idol. If they lived in the north, it was Hutton; and the dashing Denis Compton claimed the rest. There may have been the odd one who put Edrich or Washbrook on a pedestal, but in those days non-conformity was not encouraged and such allegiances were mostly kept a secret. Wicket-keepers, as a breed apart, were allowed to have a soft spot for Godfrey Evans, but without television replays to illustrate their skills, bowlers, except for the bounding leg-spinner Doug Wright, had little following, being simply there to set the game in motion. In our household it was accepted that Gover ran faster than he bowled, though on what grounds nobody explained, and I never had the chance – that is, by watching from behind the arm – to see what a great bowler Alec Bedser was. (Aspiring games-players are so lucky now, being able to soak up techniques a few feet from the television screen, not to mention the practitioners themselves, who can learn what they're doing wrong.)

As a southerner living within an hour or so of Lord's, I was well within Compton's magnetic field. But at first he wasn't even on my short-list. Thinking back over more than four decades, it comes as a surprise that despite coming from a cricket-loving family my first awareness that the game was played on a wider stage than our front lawn seems to have stemmed not from listening but from reading. I'm sure it can't be true. Bradman was too great a scourge of England not to have been a regular topic at the breakfast table, especially in 1936-37 when news of his match-winning efforts in the last three Tests would have been coming through by wireless at about the time we ate. But there it is; like so many conversations since, no doubt including far too many in the last few months, I haven't the faintest recollection of a word of them.

To the best of my belief, then, the source of my new knowledge

Denis Compton

was the issue of *The Cricketer*, probably the Winter Annual, which contained the report, and still more captivating, the score-board, of the Oval Test of 1938. England 903 for 7 declared, Hutton 364, and Australia beaten by an innings and 579! Conditioned to look on 20 as a pretty useful score, as probably it was against five competitive big sisters and a brother ten years my senior bowling with a cricket ball, the figures made my head swim every time I looked at them, which was often. An innings and 579 – wow! And the fact that Bradman and Fingleton both appeared as 'Absent hurt' did nothing to dilute my pleasure since consciously at least I'd never heard of them. Soon I memorised the score-board's other vast statistics: Leyland 187, Hardstaff 169 not out, Fleetwood-Smith 1 for 298; Heavens, what a rabbit! To begin with, inevitably, Hutton was my god: 364 in an innings lasting 13 hours and 20 minutes were figures hardly graspable. But my father, whose word was law, dismissed him as a mere pot-hunter and Leyland, of whose sturdy Yorkshire qualities he much approved, replaced him as my idol. Hammond's 59 paled into insignificance in that galaxy and as for Paynter 0 and Compton 1 – well, only the fact that they were Englishmen spared them from being lumped with Fleetwood-Smith as palpable no-hopers.

By then, though, it was wartime. Although that *Cricketer* must have been knocking round the house since soon after it was published, it can't have been till 1939 or 1940 that I was old enough to take it in – as far as Test cricket was concerned too late to do anything but dream about it until the war was over. Nevertheless, big cricket of a kind was still being played at Lord's – looking back it's remarkable how much there was of it considering the way the war was going – and finally, on 6 September, 1941, the great day dawned. My brother, home on leave, was to take me on the 355 Green Line coach to see Maurice Leyland bat at Lord's.

I never found out which member of the family was to blame for that benighted choice. My record on Green Lines was appalling: I turned green at the very thought of one. Sure enough, I was feeling sick by Radlett and retching by the time we got to Elstree. My brother kept saying 'Only another half an hour to go' but in Mill Hill it was either a scramble for the exit or the technicolour yawn. His face black with hatred, my brother dragged me out. Abused and dazed, I found myself on Mill Hill Station waiting for the stopper to St Pancras when, if someone had been thinking straight, we could have been already there on a fast train from St Alban's. How we got to Lord's remains a mystery, except that it can't have been by taxi or I would have vomited again. A.B. Sellers, the Yorkshire captain, was clean bowled by Todd of Kent with the first ball I ever saw there, but my heart was in my boots. Leyland was already out for 42. However, my brother had regained his humour. Sgt-Inst Compton was the one he'd come to see. . . and he was not out 51.

We sat in 'A' Stand, tatty old predecessor of the present Warner Stand, and were among a crowd of more than 10,000 which watched Compton complete a flashing hundred. Then, on one of his innumerable sorties down the pitch, he missed at last and was stumped by Maxwell, bowled Todd for 114. Intoxicating though the innings was – apart from Sellers' first ball the only thing I remember of the cricket – the manner of its ending affected me for years. It wasn't until 1973, when Denis turned out for an old England XI against Rachel Heyhoe's England women in a match organised by the *Evening Standard* at The Oval, that I could watch him bat without an element of terror. Two decades post-knee, plumpish, and well into his 50s, those heart-stopping advances down the pitch were a thing of the past and at last there was no fear of a stumping! It was his first knock for years, but after one rather nervous jab, his bat made its rich noise of his heyday. He scored 29 in six or seven overs and, like Hutton and Reg Simpson, showed that great players never lose their gift of timing.

In the war years, my loyalty had to stand the strain of many strong counter-attractions. Denis had been spirited away to India by some crackpot at the War Office and in his absence Edrich, Hammond, Robertson and Miller held centre stage. Hammond, still majestic, made 100 in each innings in the first match in which I ever saw him play – England versus the Dominions – in the same tremendous game Miller got his 185, including the ferocious, rifled six off Hollies that chipped brickwork above the England dressing-room. Edrich's catapulting bowling action, generating what to young eyes was unimaginable pace, made a deep impression, and it added to his lustre that he won a DFC, flying more missions than any other bomber pilot. However, although it was 1946 before I saw Compton bat again, his 114 had captured me.

There was the same infectious gaiety about his cricket, the same
warmth and boyishness as Ian Botham has, and before him Gary
Sobers. For all three, cricket was, or is, their living. But the secret
of their vast appeal was that they seemed, or seem to play the game
for fun. Keith Miller and Ted Dexter, both amateurs, were others
of the genre. Though there was never any doubting their will to
win, nor their courage, determination seldom coarsened into ruth-
lessness – never in the case of Compton. Even Botham in his
basest moments remains a chivalrous opponent.

Nobody could hope to capture the spirit of Compton's cricket
more sweetly than R.C. Robertson-Glasgow, writing in the 1948
Wisden of the great deeds of Denis and Bill Edrich the year before.
'They seem to be playing not only in front of us and for us, but
almost literally with us.' Well, since they shared 7,000 runs that
glorious summer, you could say they were entitled to enjoy themselves. But Denis didn't have to be riding on the crest of a wave to
communicate enjoyment: of all the times I saw him play, the
innings I remember best was a ridiculous 19 against Leicestershire
at Lord's in the mid-50s, when he was past his best. He strolled in
when Munden was making runs quite hard to score, bowling slow
left-arm spin to slip, gulley and a strong defensive offside field
with four men saving singles and another on the boundary. After a
cursory inspection, Denis began light-heartedly resetting it.
Crack – four to long-off over mid-off's head: one of the offside
fielders took fresh station on the boundary. Crack – four to
long-on over mid-on's head: gulley was despatched to plug the
hole. Denis chopped a two through where he'd been, drilled
Munden first bounce against the sight-screen before either adja-
cent fielder could move, picked up a few singles, then missed a
straight one and was bowled. It was like sitting down to dinner at
the Ritz and being flung into Piccadilly after the hors d'oeuvre.
Intensely irritating – but different. A great part of Compton's
charm was that no two innings were the same. And it wasn't only
my generation that fell under his spell. Ian Peebles' biography
might have been written by a doting uncle, while in his *Denis
Compton: a Cricket Sketch*, Jim Swanton told a story, so much in
character there is no doubt of its veracity, that precisely reflected
the hero's sunny nature.

'One afternoon Denis came in from batting at the tea interval, and was enduring with his usual indulgence the shafts of genially abusive humour which are a long tradition of the Middlesex dressing-room. Somebody, probably Walter Robins, said: "It's a funny thing a strong chap like you can't drive the ball straight. We never see you hit it over the bowler's head". Denis said: "Yes it is funny; look out for the third ball bowled after tea". A few minutes afterwards the third ball bowled came whistling straight and true into the Members' seats in front of the pavilion, and as the umpire was signalling "six", Denis waved his bat cheerfully to his companions.' There was more than a touch of Botham in that response, though in the latter's case the challenge he would have to answer might be to hit a backhand sweep for six!

Swanton paid Compton the compliment in that sketch of doubting whether 'any game in any period has thrown up anyone to match his popular appeal in the England of 1947-49' and even now it's hard to think of more than three – Botham, Jimmy Greaves and Bobby Charlton – who could be put up as a rival. To his young fans, the years of new-found bliss began in 1946. For though he failed to make a Test hundred against India, he made ten in first-class cricket and with 2,403 runs began making up the six years lost to war. In four home seasons, plus two hours, he scored 14,641 runs with 60 hundreds. The extraordinary affection he inspired in young and old was shown in 1949 when his benefit match, Middlesex versus Sussex in the Whitsun game at Lord's, was watched by 55,000, Denis making 182. Had Middlesex invested the resultant £12,258 with greater wisdom – and the odd horse here and there had justified his faith in them – he might today be almost as prosperous as his friend and fellow scribe Sir Leonard Hutton. Instead, not that it ever seemed to bother him, the bulk of it was lost.

In Australia in 1946-47, MCC's first post-war tour, disappointment was initially rife, tons of runs against the states being little compensation for failures in the first three Tests. With Hammond a shadow of his former self at the age of 43, the long and short of England's batting was Hutton, Washbrook, Edrich and Compton, and they were overpowered by the magnificent attack of which Lindwall and Miller were the spearhead. Caught on a sticky wicket, they lost at Brisbane by an innings and 332, and the second Test by an innings and 33 at Sydney, where Bradman

and Barnes both scored 234. Though a draw in Melbourne followed, six innings had brought Denis a bagatelle of 116. Then –
ecstasy. Demoted a place to number five at Adelaide, he made 147
and 103 not out and with Evans saved the match in the epic stand
for the ninth wicket in which the wicket-keeper went 95 minutes
before scoring. It was the dawn of Denis' dazzling 1947 when –
proof of the marvellous sureness of his striking – he scored 3,816
runs, and 18 hundreds, with one bat, a magic wand of 2lb 2oz, to
beat long-standing records by Tom Hayward and Jack Hobbs.
For the hero, bare-headed and burnished brown by weeks of
blazing sunshine, it was one long glorious frolic with the Compton
sweep, the Compton cover-drive, the Compton hook, adorning
every sports page, while on countless hoardings the handsome
Compton features, tousled hair unnaturally becalmed, smiled
down as an advertisement for Brylcreem – for a fee of £200 a year!
Against South Africa he made four hundreds in the Tests and
more than 1,000 runs in all, and one five-week spell in May and
June had five hundreds and five fifties in 11 innings – 1,169 runs
for ten times out. The sun shone and bowlers of all types became
his playthings. The sweep, because it was unique to him – he hit it
very fine and with bat nearer straight than horizontal – was his
most famous stroke; but his own favourite, and the despair of
bowlers, was the cover-drive, which by a late turn of the wrists he
could hit behind square as powerfully as to cover's right.

The photograph of a smiling Denis, bat aloft, returning to the
Hastings pavilion after overtaking Hobbs' 16 hundreds – inevitably against the hapless South Africans – remains one of the most
vivid memories of that perfect summer. Yet even then he hadn't
had enough. For Middlesex, the County Champions, against the
Rest of England over four days at The Oval, he signed off with a
flourish by scoring 246 – the innings in which, slipping as he
danced down the pitch to drive Tom Goddard, he started the long
saga of his knee. It went almost without saying that the ball still
went for four, clipped to leg as he tumbled to the ground. If the
injury lessened his mobility, however, the score-book failed to
show it. In 1948 he batted for seven hours at Trent Bridge to score
184 against Bradman's invincible Australians, added 145 at Old
Trafford after being hit on the forehead by a Miller bouncer, and
on MCC's tour to South Africa that winter put Benoni on the map

by making 300 in three hours. As late as 1950, when the knee was to cost him half the cricket season, he played for Arsenal in the FA Cup final and had a foot in the second of Reg Lewis' goals that beat Liverpool 2-0.

If I was probably no longer starry-eyed, I was still prepared to risk my job for Denis when, in 1957, I tarried at Lord's until he reached his hundred in his farewell match. 'And where have you been, might I ask?' enquired my then sports editor as I puffed into the Express building 40 minutes late. I told him, smugly, I'd been watching Compton make his final hundred. 'I could sack you for that', he threatened. But I was painless. 'Go ahead,' I said, 'it would be worth it.' He didn't. So that story had a happy ending too.

Keith Miller

PETER SMITH

The picture on the back page of the morning newspaper was probably no more than three columns wide and four inches deep but it seemed to fill the complete area, leaving no room for headlines, stories or adverts. As cricket pictures go these days, it was nothing extraordinary, either, yet the whole strength, personality and magnetic appeal of the man came leaping out. It was taken from fine-leg and showed Keith Ross Miller with his left knee bent, his right knee almost on the ground. The last few inches of his bat could be seen over his left shoulder – those shoulders appeared to fill the whole frame, with broad back tapering down to narrow waist, his face caught in profile as his eyes followed the ball that had cleared the mid-wicket boundary by yards. The photograph was one of many such pictures that could have been taken that day as the 1948 Australians played Leicestershire. They would all have demonstrated Miller's power, for he dominated the Australian innings by making 202 runs, the crowd quickly forgiving him as he strode to the crease at the fall of the first wicket when they had expected Don Bradman, the man they had come to see, to emerge.

Miller became my cricketing hero that day. My love affair with the game had just started to blossom – I was 12 years old with dreams of playing for my country, having just broken into the school second team playing with boys two or three years older than myself. If I was going to have a future in the game as a player, Keith Miller ruined it for me then. Or rather, the picture did. I could bat pretty well, at least good enough to go in at number five in schoolboy cricket. Off-spinning was my speciality, however, until that picture. I never turned another ball after that, even when I went back to off-spinning some three or four years later, having discovered I had no chance of ever becoming another Miller because I could never bowl fast enough, straight enough to

Keith Miller

copy my hero. But it was fun trying. I became a devoted Miller
follower for the rest of the 1948 season although he never produced another innings like the one at Grace Road which prompted
me to become a cricket watcher rather than a cricket reader.

I followed his every deed when he returned to England in 1953
and again in 1956, thrilled by the sight of Ray Lindwall; his grace,
his pace and his ability to swing the ball when flat out yet annoyed
whenever he ran through an England side, denying K.R. the
chance to do the same in their new ball partnership as effective as
any the game has produced. To me, Keith Miller – born in a
Melbourne suburb called Sunshine in November, 1919 – was
everything a cricketing hero should be – tall, broad-shouldered,
handsome, a batsman who could destroy the finest bowling when
he was in the mood, a fast bowler who could be as dangerous as any
other around at the time when he fancied, a slip catcher with
amazing reflexes. A man who lived life to the full. A generous
man.

He had long retired by the time I first met him, but he was all
the things I had imagined him to be when he first captured my
imagination. Some years later I took my son – then aged ten – to
Lord's, where I was covering a John Player League match. K.R.
was reporting the same game and met my son when he called at the
Press box to collect me at the close of play. We talked for a few
minutes and, as we departed, K.R. suddenly pulled a ten-pound
note from his pocket, thrust it in my hand and said 'Buy him a bat
from me'. That was typical of K.R., and the bat remains in the
Smith home today.

I never asked him the truth about two of the stories I'd heard
about his playing days because, had he denied them, it would have
shattered the image I had built up as a youngster. One concerned
the benefit match for Cyril Washbrook which the Australians
agreed to play in 1948 at Old Trafford. The wicket was suspect,
the Lancashire batting, with the exception of Jack Ikin's, being
wrecked by the Australian attack. Although bruised by more than
than one delivery that got through his guard, Ikin struggled
bravely and stubbornly to build a Lancashire score and had
reached 99 when the new ball became due. Bradman, with whom
Miller was to clash on more than one occasion, threw the new ball
to K.R., who immediately tossed it back again. 'That guy

deserves a century. I don't want to be responsible for getting him out now', he said. Bradman instead called up Lindwall who had no such respect for Ikin's gallantry and promptly dismissed him one short of a century so richly deserved.

The other story concerned an incident when Miller had moved from Melbourne to Sydney and was captain of New South Wales in a game at Sydney, a ground he loved in the same way he adored Lord's. K.R. was late arriving, so late he was still tucking in his shirt as he led his team out into the field. He was halfway to the middle when he was reminded by a colleague he had not nominated a 12th man and there were actually 11 players following him out. Without a pause in his stride Miller called out 'All right, one of you guys disappear', or words to that effect.

Even if the events did not take place exactly the way the stories were told to me, I suspect that there is a strong element of truth in both. He wanted to enjoy his cricket and wanted others to enjoy the game with him. He was not a player who took runs or wickets for personal glory or to improve his own statistics. He had no need to. They were impressive enough by the time he finished, his international record establishing him as one of the finest all-rounders the game has produced.

Starting in 1945 against New Zealand, he scored 2,958 runs from his 55 Test appearances, with seven centuries and an average of 36.97. As a fast bowler he took 170 wickets at an average of 22.97, taking ten wickets in a match on one occasion and five wickets in an innings on seven occasions. That is not all. He also took 35 catches in Test matches, making the most difficult appear easy even when they were inches from the ground, despite the fact that he often appeared to be standing up straight with his hands in his pockets when the bowler was actually delivering the ball. The most striking quality about K.R. was that things always appeared to be happening when he was on the field of play. You could never ignore him; you could not afford to take your eyes off him for a moment. There was no spite in him although he played hard for his country, angering crowds across the world by delivering vicious bouncers, sometimes on the most docile of pitches and by running only a few yards. That, for me, was the appeal of this man. Cricket was never dull when he was around. It was perhaps because he never wanted to take his fast bowling skills seriously

that he could laugh, joke, improvise so successfully. A tennis ball
– even a table-tennis ball – were known to mysteriously appear
instead of a cricket ball when he finished charging in at the end of a
run-up, conservative compared with those used today by bowlers
half Miller's pace. He claimed more than one Test wicket with a
perfectly delivered leg-break, suddenly turning in his trek back to
his mark and delivering off half-a-dozen paces. Yet to see Miller
coming in off half-a-dozen paces was no guarantee that a leg-break
was to follow. With his strength, his bouncer off such a short run
could be as vicious as the one from his full run-up. Some people
could argue that to turn suddenly and bowl off only a third of the
normal run is gamesmanship, against the spirit of the game, but,
in those circumstances, batsmen always have the option of pulling
away from the crease, claiming that they are not ready. Once they
faced up to a delivery from Miller, they had to take the consequences. It was not always pretty. When victory mattered, when his
country's cricketing reputation was at stake – as opposed to his
own, for he did not worry unduly about figures – he could prove as
nasty as any other fast bowler around at his time.

His wartime service in England from 1942 to 1945, flying with
the Royal Australian Air Force, left him with a strong affection for
most things British – he took the chance to extend his liking of
classical music and poetry – as well as many close friends. Denis
Compton, Bill Edrich and Godfrey Evans were three of his closest
(no doubt partly due to their passion for horse racing which
matched Miller's) among the England players he came across, yet
he never had any qualms about dishing out bouncers to them,
even encouraging Lindwall to do the same in the immediate
post-war years when they were both young, fresh and repaid
England for the 'Bodyline' tour of Australia in 1932-33.

Yet, strangely, Miller never wanted to be a bowler. He got into the
Victoria state side, purely as a batsman, before the Sheffield
Shield competition was suspended because of the war, and never
attempted to bowl. It was only when the Australian side composed
of servicemen played a series of victory matches against England –
composed mainly of proven Test players – in England in 1945 and
found themselves short of a strike bowler that Miller was encouraged to seriously take up the ball, and only then because others in
the side thought he was large enough with his wide shoulders to

look the part. They soon discovered he was a natural. For a while
he enjoyed the sensation, especially during the early years of his
famous partnership with Lindwall, which was first formed against
New Zealand in 1945 and lasted until 1956 against Pakistan when
Miller's knee troubles forced him to give up. As a partnership,
they took 370 wickets in 13 series, Lindwall finishing with 200
wickets – he was to take 228 in all – always having the advantage of
the wind.

Yet, after they had destroyed England in 1948, taking 40 wickets between them, Miller began to tire of his role. From then on he
was always trying to give it up, starting each summer series in
Australia by saying he would like to concentrate on batting, but
always persuaded to keep going by colleagues stressing his value to
his New South Wales side or the fact that his country needed him.
Just how successful Miller might have been; how many more than
the 170 Test wickets he finished with would have come his way if
he had had the choice of ends is pure guesswork, but a study of his
record demonstrates his importance to Australia at the time and
supports the belief that he needed a challenging target to bring out
the best in him. Of his 170 Test wickets, no less than 100 were
batsmen ranked one to five in the order. Tail-enders were not for
knocking over – unless they happened to be threatening
Australia's control. This theory is also supported by the fact that
he took five or more wickets in a Test innings on only seven
occasions – a small number when measured against the figures of,
say, Ian Botham – suggesting that having played his part in
removing the heart of the opposition batting he lost interest,
leaving others to supervise the mopping-up operations.

Understandably, for a youngster who grew up under the influence of Bill Ponsford, who lived near Miller in Melbourne, and
Bill Woodfull, the Australian captain who taught at Miller's
school, batting was his first love. While many wonder just how
many wickets he would have taken if he had been the senior fast
bowler for Australia, others wonder just how many runs he might
have scored if the demands of bowling had not interfered with his
batting. He was regarded as a reliable and steady middle-order
batsman during his schooldays and on his entry into state cricket
via the South Melbourne club.

It was not until after he returned to Australia following the war years, when he lived many of his days expecting them to be his last, that he became known as something of a cavalier, particularly after switching from Melbourne to Sydney, a city he loved just as he loved London. With his frame he was always powerful, almost cruel, on anything that could be pulled through the mid-wicket area although he was never so sure against the bouncers and largely ignored the hook. Yet he could drive the ball through the covers off the front foot as sweetly as anybody else of his day, a stroke of technical perfection.

His love affair with the English crowds in general, and those who flocked to Lord's in particular, started in 1945. He scored three centuries at Lord's that summer, the first for The Dominions against England, the other two in the Victory Test series. He seldom failed at Lord's after that, scoring his one true Test century in England there in 1953 when making 109. He was attempting to concentrate more and more on his middle-order batting then, yet the Australians would never permit him to give up the ball entirely. He was in his mid-30s when he had one of his most successful series as an all-rounder, helping the Australians beat the West Indies 3-0 in the Caribbean. Miller finished that Test series with 20 wickets, the same number as Lindwall, and also scored three centuries, two of them in Kingston, Jamaica. A year later in England he had his most successful series – in terms of figures – as a bowler, taking 21 wickets although back and knee ailments were starting to worry him.

But Miller's career is not one to be measured in terms of runs scored or wickets taken. His appeal was his personal magnetism. He was a player to be seen in person and not viewed on a television screen, and so he could pull spectators through the gates. People loved him, and he loved people. The friendships Miller made as a player lasted for life. With his ability, he could afford to be generous on the field. When he retired from the game to concentrate on writing and broadcasting, he continued to be generous in life as well.

I remember him in the West Indies in 1967-68 when he was covering England's tour. West Indies fast bowler Charlie Griffith, never a man to rouse any sympathetic feelings as a player, was coming towards the end of his career, struggling to make any impact during the first Test in Trinidad. Griffith's performance deserved criticism and Miller was not slow to deliver it. When he finished his report he went back to the bar at the Queen's Park Oval where Griffith was also having a drink. Miller immediately put an arm round Griffith and said: 'Charlie, don't read me in the papers tomorrow'. That was typical of Miller the man, and my hero. It was the way he always acted.

Ray Lindwall & Neil Harvey

DAVID FRITH

It took a lot of sorting out over the years before I knew who were my durable cricket heroes, for there has been much competition for my eager admiration and affection, from teenage years onward. Many nights, as I lay waiting for sleep to come, the 'film' I ran through my mind showed Denis Compton and myself taking the score from 20 for 3 to well over 300. Only marginally was the best of the stroke-play my partner's. Then Len Hutton's delicate poise – quite apart from his average of 88 in the 1950-51 Tests – persuaded me to assume his personality and straight bat in the marathon international contests on the strip of coarse lawn at the front of the house. Alec Bedser's skill and mighty stamina impressed deeply; but he was too hefty a man to mimic successfully. Then came Arthur Morris – principally because I was attending his old school in Sydney, but also because he was patently such a *nice* man. Keith Miller was too awesome, larger than real life, beyond emulation. It was only years later that the understanding dawned that here was the ultimate in sporting gladiators, nonchalant, bold and chivalrous. Probably the only bloke in Sydney who was aping Miller in full seriousness at that time was young Richie Benaud.

Two Australian cricketers of that time, though, were idolised by many thousands. It was a pity that the idolatry had to be on a shared basis. But it was firmly founded, and for me, I have since discovered, perpetual in its nature. I have seen them both recently, playing fun-nostalgia cricket when comfortably old enough to be grandfathers. The sight of them out there in the middle tended to choke me, for those two no longer slim figures stood for the iniquities of Time, which slunk away with their youth, my youth, and, conceivably, your youth.

Ray Lindwall was the pride of our alley. That he was the world's greatest fast bowler and represented New South Wales and

Ray Lindwall

Australia seemed only slightly more important than the fact that
he played for St George, our district club. Bradman and O'Reilly
had played for St George before the war, and now we had Lindwall
and Morris, with one of my under-16 team-mates, Norm O'Neill,
already also showing signs of genius. Many things about Ray
Lindwall appealed to me: his easy-going manner; no trace of
swank. Nor was he actually a physically intimidating giant. Most
of all, there was his bowling action, the cruising, shoulder-rolling,
menacing run and precision delivery, billowing trouser-legs
spread wide, trigger right arm sweeping through low in a blur,
leaving him with hair aflop, sleeve hanging loose. Carefully I
practised that action, every developing movement mapped out
like a ballet sequence. Many, many years later, when I was still
trying to pitch leg and take the off-stump, remarks about the low
arm were meant to disparage. Yet what my friends failed to realise
was that the 'low arm' was the very link that gratified. However
futile the rest of my efforts to emulate Lindwall, the roundarm
sling was the mark of the freemasonry – even if it had only a
one-way flow.

Only the weakest boys refrain from approaching their heroes. I
moved in closer, evening by evening, at the back of the Sydney
Cricket Ground pavilion. Autographs bred short conversations
. . . and then a request for a lift home with him, delivered so softly
as to be a whimper he did not comprehend. But one night the
question was audible, and the reply came: 'Sure!'

The journey to the match had begun as usual after school: an
uphill walk from Central Station started under a mushroom cloud
of alcoholic fume from the brewery, wound past the loading bays
of the *Daily Mirror*, where I was soon to start my working life, and
where the smell of newsprint clamped my very soul, then through
the old terraced streets of Surry Hills. At last the view flattened
out across the expanse of Moore Park, and there were the cream
and green stands of the SCG on the horizon. The pace quickened.
Just short of the turnstiles it was possible to get a glimpse of the
score-board on the Hill. It was always a better sight when the
yellow arrow marker indicated that Lindwall was in action. There
was I, shuffling, part-mesmerised, through the shadows beneath
the old Brewongle Stand; and there was he, out in the dazzling
sunlight, face pink, hair ruffled, and cheeks taut from effort.

It was best to sit up in the Sheridan Stand, to watch the glistening red ball burn a path away through space, swerving to the left and leaving the mug batsman fanning at nothing; or ducking to the right and clacking against the stumps, usually removing one of them for a thrill equalled in all sport only by Randolph Turpin's knock-out left hook. Lindwall's bumper, used, on the whole, sparingly, caused a rippling murmur, broken by a few exclamations from the Hill. And all this was even more dramatic when he bowled from the Paddington end – in effect at me. Effort given, he would struggle into his sweater, often losing half his shirt-collar; then the loose cap was flicked on at an undisciplined angle, and he would shuffle off to his position in the gulley.

A few hours later, showered and with the lost body-fluid well and truly replaced, Ray Lindwall, in sports-jacket and suede shoes, emerged from the rear of the pavilion, crossed the lawn, and found a starry-eyed young chap waiting by his Holden. He was annoyingly modest. He obviously needed to unwind, for he could never be persuaded to explain just how he had got Stollmeyer or Weekes or McGlew out. It was a time to discuss history and geography and biology as we sped round the lip of Botany Bay. It was ludicrous. At first, it was all I could do to speak at all, having taken so much out of myself in engineering the lift. How I used to wish that a gasket would blow, forcing us to stop, and extending the journey time. My classmates wouldn't believe me the first time I had a lift in Lindwall's car. There seems nothing sensational about it now, but in 1952 it was like being invited into Napoleon's carriage or Bing Crosby's limousine.

Carlton was three miles from Hurstville where Ray had lived since his own boyhood. There he had bowled a tennis ball at a kerosene tin in the roadway in an effort to attract the great Bill O'Reilly as he made his way home from work. Now, while there was still some light, I would grab my tennis ball and do my Lindwall look-alike, though there was no one there to watch me, except sometimes my father, who thought I ought to ping the tin every ball, and somehow failed to appreciate the subtleties of the out-swinger – easily achieved with a tennis ball – and the bumper, which had to be retrieved from a grumpy neighbour's garden. We almost got Ray Lindwall into the house once. As he set me down, Mum waved, called cheerily, and told him the pot of tea was ready

to pour. But he leant out of the car window and excused himself –
adenoidally, shyly, nicely.

Then came the final car ride, though thank goodness I didn't
know it. It was all over. Again, I could only watch from the distant
stand and go home by train. He took his 100th wicket against
England before my very eyes, and he played on until he was 38,
finishing with a then-record 228 Test wickets for Australia. A lot
of Sydneysiders had been disappointed when he married and went
to Queensland – not disappointed that he married, of course, but
upset that he had 'defected'. Looking back, I wonder if it was pure
coincidence when, a couple of years later, I went to Queensland
(enforcedly, admittedly, with the Royal Australian Air Force) and
also ended up blissfully married to a Queensland girl. And just to
ram home the blind, helpless identification with my hero, allied
this time to sweet chance, within the year I had taken 6 for 20 for
St George as we got Randwick out for 52. If those figures have no
significance, perusal of the Oval Test match score of 1948 will
reveal all. Few days have been so cherished.

My other knight in shining armour? He was younger than
Lindwall, smaller and batted left-handed. Neil Harvey always had
sunlight gleaming across his cricket. Even to someone as imma-
ture as I, he represented youthfulness, audacity and unlikely
command – unlikely because of his size. He always looked a boy
among men. He was not strident or grossly dominant. Those
qualities would not have appealed, anyway, to a youth who himself was unsure about life.

Harvey's dark head was always inclined, as if in partial apology,
as he walked briskly and neatly out through the gateway. He
hardly ever wore a cap, that earnest token of shelter; all his
accoutrements were white or cream: he was one of the first to
adopt white batting-gloves, and bats were then devoid of garish
flashes and stripes. He always seemed too small to survive, but
when he started to move, his genius shone. Those darting little
feet took him across the crease or down the pitch, always with a
neatness of execution that had the same effect on the spectator as
rounding a corner in a gallery and seeing a brilliant canvas or
sculpture. Except that Harvey was seldom still. In his batting,
flourish and discipline harmonised. After his torrent of Test
centuries, particularly against the South Africans, and his brave

Neil Harvey

92 not out against the fire of Tyson and Statham when the other
Australians looked third-raters, news of his pair of noughts in
Laker's Test at Manchester in 1956 was dumbfounding. Still, he
did captain Australia to victory in the Lord's Test of 1961.

There was one very odd thing about the Harvey-worship.
Whenever I heard the clear, glad sound of a Guy Mitchell record-
ing on the radio, I pictured Neil Harvey. Psychologists might have
an explanation. Anyway, Guy Harvey – or Neil Mitchell – or
whatever his name was – batted and sang me through the carefree
summers of my teenage years.

Around 1962 I found I was actually due to play against Neil
Harvey in a first-grade match. All the old Cardus-type prayers
were revived during the tossing and turning of the night before the
match: let Neil make a century, and let's get them all out for 135.
No one ever morally anticipated a Bill Lawry innings in that
fashion. Harvey scored only ten, and I could have throttled our
off-spinner for bowling him. But at least I had chased a back-cut
almost to the fence, and thrown in as they completed a third run.
On the second day, Harvey bowled me with a curving full-toss. I
didn't want to get out, I swear it.

There was always something 'singing' about Harvey's batsmanship, and even when he had to fight, with runs coming slowly, the
music was never entirely silenced. He was a prince of sunshine,
and looked as alien to the environment when rugged up in sweat-
ers at damp, dark Bradford or drab Kennington Oval as the
tanned, short-sleeved Beach Boys when they performed their
escapist musical magic in wintry North London. Harvey was
summer and eternal youth.

There should be no comparisons. Mozart isn't better than
Haydn; nor Dickens than Nabokov. Since Lindwall, there have
been Hall and Holding, Procter and Lillee and Thomson and
Willis and Kapil Dev. But I can still picture, every bit as clearly,
Ray Lindwall going through his loosening exercises at the extrem-
ity of his run-up, while the batsman tried to look calm and
unaffected even though sometimes it was as if he were tied to a
stake, watching his executioner test the bolt action of his rifle. As
was said more than once, with vividly good reason, Lindwall
moved in to bowl as if on castors.

Lindwall and Harvey were to be seen again playing against 'Old

England' at The Oval in 1983. Ray was good for only three overs off a short run. He was, after all, past 60. The action was the genuine old article, if in slow motion. The arm was no lower than in the old days. Someone remarked that it couldn't have been anyway. He operated from the same end as the lean demon of 35 years before, when he took that 6 for 20. Neil Harvey patrolled the covers in a threatening manner which owed much to legend, though there was one memorable pick-up and flat throw. When he batted, Time's ravages were hardly evident. The drive still worked, and the cut which had helped him towards 21 Test centuries was in good functional order. And as the ball blurred its way to the cover boundary, deep inside my head the strains of 'Sparrow in the Treetop' jumbled with 'My Truly, Truly Fair'.

Godfrey Evans

HENRY BLOFELD

When I was ten years old I gave up a potentially erratic career as a leg-spinner and donned a pair of wicket-keeping gloves because one of the regular wicket-keepers in the first game at my school was injured. I suppose I must have shown some sort of aptitude for I was allowed to continue and I did my best to learn all I could about the art. By the end of the summer term in 1950, the greatest man on earth as far as I was concerned was Godfrey Evans. He had replaced Denis Compton by the length of a street.

My mother and father took me to watch one day's play of the second Test match at Lord's, England versus West Indies, in 1950. I was mesmerised by Evans, and from that moment on, I spent all my waking life trying to imitate the great man. I can still see in my mind's eye on that far distant day at Lord's the blur of movement as he ran to meet a bad throw-in and take it on the full toss. Then there was the thrilling, ear-splitting appeal for a catch behind with the ball thrown far in the air in his moment of triumph. There was, too, the tigerish satisfaction of the appeal to the square-leg umpire as the bails were whipped off and the umpire was asked to give his views on a possible stumping. Evans was like a coiled spring all the time. But probably the single movement which fascinated me more than any other was the way in which, when he was standing back and took the ball in those gloves with exciting red rubber faces, he despatched it to gulley in the same movement as he accepted it into his hands. It was all done with such an infectious flourish. I am sure I was unable to appreciate fully the tremendous skills necessary to stand up to the stumps to Alec Bedser, especially when he went across to leg to take that in-swinger, but it was magnetic and I was unable to take my eyes off my hero for a single second. When my mother and father suggested an early lunch a major family row ensued.

All I ever wanted to do after that day was to own a pair of

Godfrey Evans

red-faced wicket-keeping gloves, which seemed to me to be the
last word in just about everything. Of course, if I was going to
imitate Godfrey Evans, first I had to look like him. The problem
now was that I and approximately 70 other little boys at Mr Fox's
establishment in Sunningdale had had it drummed into our heads
that swank was wholly unacceptable. We had to be modest in
everything, and what was good enough for Godfrey Evans was
most palpably not good enough for little show-offs aged ten. On
my 11th birthday I was given a copy of Evans' biography, *Behind
the Stumps*, which I devoured at breakneck speed. I became word
perfect when it came to the tips to young wicket-keepers. There
was a photograph of a leg-side stumping and then of a diving catch
which made anything of Michelangelo's look like the answer to
question one. I lay awake at nights, though, wondering why
ear-splitting appeals and throwing the ball far into the air when
appealing for a catch behind should be regarded by those in charge
of my welfare as the unacceptable face of professionalism.

Then, too, they did not care much for the one aspect of Evans'
keeping that I was pretty good at. After hours, days and weeks of
practice, I felt I had really come to terms with taking the ball in my
gloves and sending it sideways to gulley all in the same satisfying
movement. I suppose polite young wicket-keepers were probably
expected to under-arm the ball back to the bowler when he was at
the end of his follow-through. But after a time, Charlie Sheep-
shanks, who ran the cricket, was prepared to turn a blind eye
when I threw the ball away to gulley.

Evans' batting also brought me a great delight and joy as he
impishly slogged fast and slow bowling alike to all parts of the
field. And then there was the wonderful occasion when I sat with
my ear glued to a wireless – they were most definitely not radios in
those days – when he almost scored 100 before lunch in a Test
match against India at Lord's in 1952. In fact, he was 98 or 96 at
the interval, and although he reached three figures immediately
afterwards, I remember taking it as a personal insult that the
umpires would not allow just one more over before going in.

To those who tried to tell me that while it was one thing to
model one's wicket-keeping on Godfrey Evans, to try to adopt his
batting style was quite another, I would point angrily to the
Adelaide Test on the Australian tour of 1946-47. In England's

second innings, Evans batted for over an hour and a half before he scored a run, making it possible for Denis Compton to score his second century of the match and England to dig themselves out of a pretty nasty hole.

I don't think I have experienced such vicarious nervousness as I did when I went into the classroom having just heard that Evans had struck his first ball mightily for four. For the next 50 minutes it was sheer agony, and then a frantic scramble back to the wireless when the class ended. Yes, we heard that Compton was still batting, but who was with him? With my heart in my mouth I waited for the score – even in those days commentators did not give the score often enough – praying fervently that England were still only five wickets down. If Evans was out, it made me slightly vindictive towards those who taught me. But then it was joy unconfined, almost delirium, when a batsman, preferably an Australian, got an inside edge and there was Evans standing back, diving far to the left down the leg-side and bringing off a catch that the commentators could only describe as miraculous.

I collected every newspaper cutting about Evans I could lay my hands on. I devoured tour books and I would endlessly re-read the bits about his brilliant diving catches down the leg-side or in front of slip. Then there was that photograph of all photographs when on the last morning at Melbourne, I think it was, Evans flashed away full length to his right to pick up an authentic leg-glance which Neil Harvey had played against Frank Tyson. Harvey was 92 and that catch virtually guaranteed victory for England. I still have my copy of A.G. 'Johnny' Moyes' book about that series, *Fight for the Ashes*, and my heart still beats just a little bit quicker when I come to the well-worn page which describes that piece of sheer brilliance. Evans claimed 219 dismissals in Test cricket and he also made 2,439 runs, with two hundreds, but these figures do not tell a millionth of the man. For me, there will never be a greater or more perfect wicket-keeper.

Oh yes, and I got those red-faced gloves eventually – when my hands were big enough to fit them. And I have to pinch myself almost daily to believe that these days I rub shoulders with Godfrey Evans and even have the temerity to call him 'Godders'. He is as good a friend and companion as he was a wicket-keeper.

Jim Laker

ROBIN MARLAR

Someone, I suppose, helped Jim Laker with his book, *Spinning Round the World*. Every author needs a sympathetic editor. He was helped not very much, I suspect: even though this was a first effort, way back in 1957. Four years before that, when we had asked him rather cheekily to come and help the Cambridge team, and been bowled over by his ready acceptance, some of us had come to realise just how much cricket was in the man. So much that it spilled out of him, to be lapped up like nectar at Fenners by undergraduates wanting to learn, to learn not only about cricket but about an already great bowler's approach and attitudes to life itself. Not all tutorials happen among the books and pipe smoke in the drawing rooms of College dons.

Little did we, the pupils, know what was in store, what *magnum opus* remained to be launched into the long-lasting world of cricket academia. In 1956, Jim Laker, having taught the significance for an attacking bowler of getting out half an opposing team, proceeded to take all ten wickets for Surrey against the Australians at The Oval. And then, as if this were not startling enough by itself, he took 19 of their wickets in the Old Trafford Test match, leaving just one crumb for his 'spin twin', Tony Lock. In his book he describes that evening, one of those classic moods which we all savour once or twice in a lifetime if we are lucky, moods that stretch all the way back to the night after Theseus slew the bull at Marathon. 'I did not get to my car until eight o'clock. And there scores of people were waiting for autographs of souvenir scorecards to be completed. Finally I headed South at about 8.30 pm – alone. I was left to myself and my own thoughts. I had to drive through the night, for I, too, was playing the next day – against the Australians! I 'phoned my wife twice en route. I knew she would be worried in case I celebrated too generously. She need not have concerned herself. My celebration "dinner" consisted of a

Jim Laker

bottle of beer and a sandwich in a pub near Lichfield. I sat in the corner of a crowded bar for 15 minutes while everyone there talked about the Test match. No one spotted me. Beyond asking me how far I had to go, the landlord said nothing. Still, I was grateful for the privacy.'

There, that is Laker the laconic at his superlative best. Those of us lucky enough to attend the same school as the celebrated Dr Johnson were taught to believe that those who are tired of London are tired of life. Many more are convinced that if our capital city is the Athens of modern Britain, then Leeds is its Sparta. You expect a man like Laker, brought up in Bradford, the very heart of British Laconia, to be a man of few words. That, in a nutshell, is why he has proved such an outstanding television commentator.

More than a year after he had placed himself firmly at the top of the most interesting table of bowlers in *Wisden* with 19 Test wickets in a single match, Jim Laker had to make a speech to the assembled Athenians. The occasion was a lunch given by *The People* newspaper. Emulating the *Daily Telegraph* in the heyday of Dr W.G. Grace, *The People* launched a shilling fund to honour the feat. Between the tumble of wickets at Old Trafford and the drawing of the cheque to be presented, Laker himself, and England, had completed a tour of South Africa. Meanwhile at Lord's, the legislators, acting in unholy alliance with, of all people, Sir Don Bradman, had destroyed one of the essential pillars of cricket, namely the right of every bowler through his captain to place the fielders to suit his style. Henceforth there were to be restrictions of fielders on the leg-side. Laker graciously accepted his cheque, laconically commented that he was 'interested to see that while I have been away, the game's lawyers have made it impossible for anyone to repeat my success'. Whereupon the Spartan spinner went off to develop a pleasant residential estate in Putney, the part of Athens in which he had chosen to settle, a place where London-based hero-worshippers can still go and stand in Laker Close, and wonder how many more Bradford bank-clerks are likely to finish up as part of our national furniture.

As for cricket, perhaps that was never again the same for Laker. There were those who thought that he became testy. He certainly produced articles that were highly critical of authority, and if some of us thought the criticism highly deserved, it was nonetheless sad to see him out of favour at The Oval for a few years, ending his days in harness in Essex alongside Trevor Bailey, another who thought straight about cricket, spoke his mind, and never captained England because of it. Such was Laker's love for the game that he went on playing until the 1974 season when he was 42, which may seem to be a great age to be playing today when only Fred Titmus bowls like Peter Pan, but it was an early enough retirement compared to the career of Tom Goddard.

Like Goddard, Laker was a bowler who had learned to slow down, not only in the pace of delivery, but in his action and indeed in every other part of his cricket. In the field he would stroll from gulley to gulley, a catcher there unlike a Benaud, athletic and swift of reflex, but one hopeful enough that something would stick. All his life he marvelled at the courage and example of his skipper, Stuart Surridge, whom he used to blame for 'walking in' from short-leg and missing catches for being too close, just as the suicidal, helmeted catchers miss them in the 1980s. In the outfield, Laker pulling on his sweater between overs seldom broke into a trot towards his place, and if he did, it was the tight, somewhat stilted run of the upright man whose joints were never gymnastically supple. Between the wickets, too, he was no sprinter, although he made valuable runs for England. His stroke-making depended on a great circular wave of the bat, such a gesture as a flamboyant conductor might make in front of an orchestra.

It was with the ball that Laker made his music. All his skill was founded on the final leap into his delivery, not an exaggerated leap you understand, but a final decisive movement which was impeccably and invariably rhythmic. Jim Laker never bowled an ugly ball, and like all great bowlers he bowled precious few bad 'uns either. He was always sideways to the batsman and always high. The left side never collapsed over the front foot as he released the ball. In all this he was so different to Tom Goddard, who showed a lot of his chest to the batsman and yet seemed to lean so far forward that he was just dropping the ball on the spot. Goddard had longer fingers than Laker, but Laker spun that cricket ball like a top. Ever since he has been somewhat scathing about the many rollers whom he has seen in the game. Indeed, in his own time, after an early and unsuccessful start against the

aforementioned Bradman, he lost his place to an even quieter
off-break bowler, Roy Tattersall, who was the ace pusher of the
seam in his day, a master bowler on wet wickets of Lancashire and
a better purveyor even than Laker of the arm ball that runs away to
the slips – the ball that made Titmus such a long-lasting artist.

Laker taught his followers to rip the fingers across the ball –
literally. His early experience had taught him that finger spinners,
black or white, right- or left-hand, were as likely to give blood as
the fast bowlers whose blood was always in their boots. These days
you seldom hear of spin bowlers missing matches because of a sore
spinning finger. Before every season the likes of Laker would
steep their hands in salt water, or some other patented solution.
Friar's balsam was a favourite of Jim's, and you wondered
whether the yellow on the first two fingers of his right hand came
from a pre-session dip or the last packet of fags. His fingers, and
those of Tony Lock, literally split deep into the thick skin, notably
at the top of the forefinger, between the first joint and the end.
You took the field with the split barely healed, knowing that it
would break open in the first over, and yet there might be 200
more balls to bowl that day. Unless they were all given a tweak,
they were unlikely to deviate. No wonder Laker used to send an
unspoken signal to Peter May, turning his arm over with an
outward and therefore much more visible move of the elbow
before intently examining, from the outside looking in, the end of
his key digit. The shorter-fingered brethren were perhaps luckier
in that circles of raw developed where the skin was thin, over the
joints themselves. Thereabouts a product was launched called
Nu-Skin, and a bottle of that applied every over, whilst it stung
like hell, at least blocked the edges of the sore where the splits
might get serious. Sometimes you could get three sores like that on
the first two fingers. Jim, I know, tried Nu-Skin, but I don't think
it helped.

By then his fingers were giving him another, even more serious
problem. Through continual spinning the fingers change shape.
Because they are also used in fielding they get bruised and may
swell. Spinning on a bruised finger can do lasting damage. So can
arthritis. Whatever the cause, once the joint is swollen not only the
pain but also the rigidity can prevent the fingers ripping across the
seam. Pace off the pitch comes from the alliance of that spin and
the perfect form of the delivery. Laker's delivery was never lost,

but there came a time when he found the role of stock bowler less than amusing. In the Surrey side there were plenty of others to bowl so that hardly mattered. Both Eric Bedser and Tom Clark could bowl better off-spinners than the first choice in many other counties.

However, year after year Laker did the business for his county. The yardstick of that was 100 wickets, then the mark for any front-line bowler worth his place. Laker hit that target no fewer than 11 times. Once he reached 166 but somehow he was not the type to reach 200 in a season, a man too laconic for that species of *annus mirabilis*. By the end he and his action had become so familiar that every mimic on the circuit could 'do a Laker'; body upright, and the left hand held high and cocked back at the wrist, which was the very special Laker trademark. Now when one sees him in or around a pavilion he is no longer smoking the inevitable cigarette. Sensibly, he heeded his heart surgeon's advice. Otherwise he is still the same old Laker, he of the measured walk and the measured words. But he was a killer with the ball and his quality came not only from his action but from one of the most finely-tuned cricketing brains of his or any other generation. It is in this combination of both physical and mental application that greatness lies. Jim Laker will for ever be the champion off-spinner.

Johnny Wardle

DEREK HODGSON

On a July afternoon in 1958 at Bramall Lane, Sheffield, Yorkshire had just bowled out Somerset for 162. Johnny Wardle, the senior professional, was resting on figures of 6 for 46 when he was told the Committee wished to see him. He put on his blazer and left, returning to the dressing-room later having lost most of the colour from his usually ruddy cheeks. He was 35, indisputably among the best five spinners in the world, and he had been sacked. When the next volume of Yorkshire cricket history comes to be written the compiler may well trace the start of the county's decline to that date, the very first crack in the façade of Lord Hawke's empire. There has not been a great spin bowler in Yorkshire since Wardle, and the very foundation of that empire lay in the continuing supremacy of her slow left-arm bowlers stretching back through Verity, Rhodes, Peel, Peate as far as 'the good-natured grin' of Ike Hodgson in the 1850s. On that one afternoon Yorkshire cut a cord that was an attachment to greatness.

Why? There was a smouldering and growing resentment at Surrey's dominance in the championship: seven firsts in seven years was too much for Yorkshiremen to swallow when it could be, and was, argued that man for man there was not a great deal between the two teams in individual ability. Inside the Committee, according to memoirs since published, the feeling was that the leadership was to blame and, wedded as the Committee were then to an amateur captain, the utmost support had to be given to the newly-appointed leader from the Bradford League, Ronnie Burnet. So when Burnet reported dissension, mostly on tactical grounds, between himself and the senior professional, there was a strong call for an example to be made, and Wardle, without warning of any kind, was sacked.

The consequences of such a catastrophic error were hidden by Yorkshire's winning of the championship in 1959, a fortuitous

Johnny Wardle

covering of the body by a snowstorm. Shaken, anxious to tell his side of the affair, Wardle sold the story to the *Daily Mail*, was removed from the MCC team to tour Australia and never played first-class cricket again. He had, he thought, ten good years left. Whatever role Wardle occupied in those ten years – and Yorkshire were to appoint a professional in Vic Wilson to follow Burnet – his value to his county would have been immense. Just as the sergeant-major is the backbone of the regiment so the senior professional, with his transmitted lore, his hoary tales of plundered runs and easy wickets, his repertoire of tricks and dodges for upsetting newcomers, is the fulcrum of the dressing-room. Had Wardle continued to play cricket until 1968, it is not too much to speculate that he might have delayed or prevented the abrupt disintegration of the 1960s side that led, in turn, to the bitter disappointments of the 1970s.

Yet in 1958 Wardle's sacking was not a surprise to those close to cricket's establishment. Johnny, beloved of small boys and idolised by adolescent cricketers, was not popular with authority. Words such as 'difficult', 'awkward', 'chip-on-the-shoulder', 'big-headed', and 'show-off' were used against him. Two Test cricketers have told me they believed Wardle had deliberately dropped catches off their bowling in order to claim the batsmen as his own victims later. It is time for a re-assessment of John Henry Wardle.

I have never met him, but that is no bad thing with heroes, for they have to preserve what the *Concise Oxford Dictionary* calls their 'superhuman qualities'. The word is Greek and antique; wise old Homer kept his distance, foreseeing that while Achilles might sulk in his tent, we would be no happier to learn that he also slurped his soup. But it is important to talk to people who knew Wardle well. Ted Lester, now Yorkshire's scorer, was a free-scoring batsman of the 1950s team – two centuries in one Roses' match! – and can remember Wardle from before he knew his name: 'There is a famous picture, dating from 1939, of George Hirst at the Headingley nets. Among the kids standing round George Herbert are, unknown to each other, E.J. Lester and J.H. Wardle'. The pair met in the Colts' team of 1946. The following year, as Yorkshire rebuilt, Lester (Scarborough) was the room-mate of J.V. Wilson (Malton) until Vic was dropped for a spell and

Wardle took his place. 'We three tended to hang about together. We were the more sober element of that team.' Lester's assessment of Wardle's playing ability is simple: 'He was a genius. Apart from having all the accepted virtues of the orthodox slow left-arm bowler, he could also bowl the chinaman and googly at a time when there were two famous Australian practitioners playing in this country, Jack Walsh and George Tribe. Johnny didn't spin the fancy stuff as much as Walsh, but he had more control and he was every bit as good a bowler as Tribe'.

Because of Yorkshire's batting strength Wardle's contribution was usually reserved for the flail for quick runs, but Fred Trueman, a fair judge of bowlers who bat, reckons that Wardle would have had several first-class hundreds had he batted up the order. As a fielder he was a conjuror close in, a man who could perform tricks with the ball, catch it and make it disappear. Pat Murphy in *The Spinner's Turn* tells of a grim Roses' match at Sheffield where Cyril Washbrook, very conscious of the occasion, was forswearing his strokes, determined to grind a century out of the old foe until, given a loose ball, he went for the pull and was caught by Wardle at short fine-leg. But so quickly was the catch executed, and the ball pocketed, with Wardle gazing earnestly at the boundary, that Washbrook was half-way through his second run before he believed he was out. Cyril was not amused.

But the crowds loved Wardle. Today, in one-day cricket, he would be a megastar, a Ray East in humour, an Essex in entertainment, a bowler who could hit prodigious sixes and bowl up to half-a-dozen different deliveries. It would be worth a mint of money to see Wardle bowling modern batsmen who, poor souls, have never seen anyone remotely like him.

Why then was such a cricketer dropped by Yorkshire and always uncertain of his England place? Ted Lester explains: 'He had a chip placed on his shoulder from his early days. At the time he was crucified by the Yorkshire press, who couldn't accept that he was different. Rhodes and Verity didn't need to bowl chinamen so why should he? Did he think he was a cut above them? And when things went wrong, as they will with any spinner, and he got some tap, they were twice as hard on him. Even when he got established in the Yorkshire side he knew the captain didn't always share his patience'. Wardle liked to explore a batsman for three or four overs, feed him a little to see how he responded. In South Africa he once had to plead with Peter May to let him stay on after John Waite had collected three easy fours. 'Please, skipper,' begged Wardle, 'he's mine next over.' And he was. On that same 1956-57 tour, given his head in the second Test in Cape Town, he took 12 for 89. Douglas Insole afterwards described it as the best bowling he'd ever seen.

That chip on the shoulder grew with England's regular preference for Tony Lock as the slow left-arm bowler in the national side, especially as Wardle firmly believed, and was confirmed in his belief when it was too late, that Lock's faster ball was illegal. It is a heart-breaking reflection on the deterioration in the quality of cricket that 30 years ago England could choose between two such brilliant bowlers. Today most Committees and captains seem to regard left-arm spinners as freaks who would be better advised to fire the ball in, seam up, at the leg-stump. One of the richest subtleties, the patient, gradual entrapment of a batsman, has been all but driven from the game.

Wardle off the field was less of a joker. Ted Lester again: 'Strange as it seems, Johnny was not unlike Geoff Boycott. A terrific professional. Very dedicated. The job always came first. Cricket was a marvellously social game in those days, before Sunday play and one-day tournaments, but Johnny was always in bed before midnight. To clown around he needed an audience, but his sense of humour was always there. We were staying at a good hotel in Cambridge when one of the young players went through four courses and declared himself still hungry. So Johnny pointed to the menu and said, "Why don't you try this? I'm told it's very tasty". The young player called over the waiter and ordered. "I'll have a plate of that, lad." The waiter blushed red and replied, "I'm afraid that's the date, sir". The menu was printed in French'.

Lester refutes allegations about dropped catches. 'I don't believe it. Johnny couldn't do that. What he could do, and did, was try something clever with the ball and fail. Those were the times when some hard words were exchanged and I've no doubt that's where those stories start. But drop a catch deliberately? Never.' Lester adds: 'Don't forget Wardle's popularity, especially with the crowd, made other players jealous which, in turn, made Wardle perhaps feel isolated. He would have been much happier under a hard captain like Brian Sellers who came down on everyone impartially. Norman Yardley was perhaps too much of a gentleman for that team. What was needed, often, was a reminder to a lot of big talents that the team came first, always'. Norman Yardley's great regret was that Yorkshire did not have a contemporary slow left-arm bowler, as good as Wardle but orthodox, so that Johnny could have been used more as a shock than a stock bowler. The rise of Bob Appleyard and Fred Trueman, both of whom could play the prima donna, added to the tensions in what Lester admits was a far from happy dressing-room.

Yet Wardle left many rich and happy memories of his career: 195 wickets at an average of 16.14 in 1955; 4 for 7, with Australia 35 for 8, at Old Trafford in 1953 and then dropped by England; in 12 years he took 1,800 wickets at an average of 18, and delighted hundreds of thousands. Ted Lester says: 'I'll never forget the tie with Leicestershire at Huddersfield. They needed one to win. Terry Spencer drove on the off-side and set off for an easy single. Johnny, who was bowling, darted towards mid-off, picked up almost nonchalantly and calmly knocked out the middle stump. Great cricket'.

Wardle always wanted to live up to being in the line of Peel, Rhodes and Verity. He loved to listen to the legends. He was proud to tell Pat Murphy of listening to Rhodes' talk of technique at Scarborough. Most of all he desperately wanted to be thought one of them. I believe he succeeded.

Fred Trueman

PETER BAXTER

A scowl at the wretched batsman. A deliberately pigeon-toed stalk back to a far distant mark, folding the right sleeve the while. (Folding it artfully, mind you, so that it will need to be refurled after the delivery.) Another scowl, scratching the run-up mark again like a bull pawing the ground, then – toes still turned in – the accelerating run to the wicket. For a fraction of a second the trigger is cocked; then the long final stride with an exaggerated drag of the right toe; a fury of arms (yes, the sleeve came down) and a schoolmaster's weary voice, 'Baxter, why don't you stick to leg-spin?'.

Yes, why should a Sussex schoolboy have imagined himself to be Yorkshire's fiery Fred? Memory, of course, distorts, but the late 1950s seem to have been bathed in a rosy glow in which Peter May's England swept all before them. Richardson and Cowdrey always seemed to have 100 on the board before the first wicket fell. But should trouble come, there was always the broad bat of Bailey or, if fireworks were called for, the merry *joie de vivre* of Evans. Then, before the deadly wiles of Laker and Lock, the opposition had to face England's champions – Statham and Trueman. They were the perfect foils for each other. Brian Statham's 'You miss, I hit' accuracy. Fred Trueman's swing and movement and the genuine pace of the pair of them. Statham's reserved nature; Trueman's boastful swagger and very presence. At what point did the raw Trueman aggression capture my youthful imagination? His bursting on the scene with India reduced to 0 for 4 wickets in his first Test – appropriately at Headingley and under a new captain, Hutton, a Yorkshireman and a professional – had happened in the mists before my cricket consciousness. I awoke to cricket with Fred already a folk hero.

Televised Test cricket was limited in the1950s as, indeed, were television sets, but maybe that gave an edge of excitement to

Fred Trueman

expeditions to County matches. At the Cheltenham Festival I first clapped eyes on those strange men from the North. Almost a foreign country indeed – Yorkshire! We saw little of Trueman, F.S. there. On a turning pitch Wardle held sway with blood-curdling appeals and Fred bowled only seven overs, but he was a stirring sight. And he was no bad model for a young boy to try to emulate. How many times since then have I heard him say, 'Cricket is a sideways-on game, sunshine'? And, if some of Fred's reminiscences have acquired the tints afforded by rose-coloured spectacles, in this anyway he was exemplary. The wildness of his aspect belied the perfection of his action.

Watching from the boundary we knew little of the comments to the batsman which accompanied the follow-through or, of course, of the legendary morning visits to the opposition dressing-room which shook the nerve of the newcomer or the faint-hearted. Most of this, though, was the extension of an impish sense of humour. And if bowling was business, batting was his – and his adoring public's – joy. We looked down the score-card: 'Oh good, True-man's in at number nine, that'll be fun'. And it was.

The batting part of life was conducted with a cheerful attitude beneath a jaunty cap. And it was no mere slog. He always turned out as competent-looking a batsman as any, but how we cheered the more extravagant strokes! His three on-driven sixes in one over off Sonny Ramadhin at Lord's in 1957 were a delightful *coup de grace* after the toil of May and Cowdrey in the first Test at Edgbaston. Three first-class hundreds provided the tangible proof of his potential for responsible batting.

Fred, the people's hero, could do anything, we all felt. How shattering it was for that same schoolboy a few years later to hear by the concealed ear-piece from a transistor radio while studying German verbs in a panelled classroom the commentary on the start of the Old Trafford Test match. Trueman bowled and four times in succession Conrad Hunte struck him to the boundary. What an indignity! But revenge was to come for Fred in that West Indian summer of 1963. From a camp of pads, bats, blazers and cricket bags under a lime tree beside a school cricket field we listened to the news from Edgbaston. Days before our nerves had been jangled as the dramatic draw in the Lord's Test reached its sensa-tional conclusion with the injured Cowdrey coming out – arm in plaster – to save the game with David Allen. Now Trueman had put England on top. The shout went up – our own game forgotten – as he ended the potentially destructive innings of Frank Worrell and won the match with a haul of 12 wickets. In the next two Tests the West Indies were to stamp the authority of Hall and Griffith on the series, winning it 3-1, but at that moment triumph was in the air and pictures of Fred in his bath and Fred with a pint adorned the papers the next day. He was always good newspaper copy.

I would like to add my name to the list of those who say 'I was there when Fred took his 300th Test wicket'. I would like to, but although I remember it clearly enough – the edge by Neil Hawke to Colin Cowdrey at slip and the congratulations from those two gentlemen which followed – I have to confess that I witnessed it only on television. That happened on the Saturday of the 1964 Oval Test match and I had been there on Friday to be lulled to sleep by Bill Lawry taking an eternity to make 94. Fred had had no success that day and my view of him was mainly of the substantial rear end ('you've got to have a big bottom to bowl fast, sunshine') at short-leg, where he lurked as the spinners wheeled away. Fred's brilliant close to the wicket fielding, in fact, exploded the myth that fast bowlers needed to be hidden in the field. Apart from making the oft-quoted remark that he did not know if anyone else would get 300 Test wickets, but 'if they do, they'll be bloody tired', Fred's achievement gave a signpost to the future, although I doubt whether anyone realised it at the time. He was brought to the radio commentary box and invited to describe one of the early overs in England's second innings, which he did with fluency and aplomb. Since that heady day the 300 mark has been passed by Lance Gibbs, Dennis Lillee and Bob Willis. I fear these triumphs have sometimes hurt Fred. They should not, as they detract not one bit from his own great record.

One further clear memory lingers with me from those days. It comes from the old Carling Single Wicket tournament at Lord's. (Incidentally, this was taken seriously enough by the BBC to afford it radio commentary). The highlight of the first round of the 1964 tournament looked likely to be W.W. Hall versus F.S. Trueman. In the 34 balls which it took Fred to capture his wicket, Hall made 45. The roles were reversed and Fred came out to face the fastest bowler in the world. Hall started to mark out a run which looked likely to start in the Long Room itself. Rising to the occasion, Fred shaded his eyes to make out his protagonist in the distance. The gesture was rewarded by Hall putting several more yards on his run. This time he turned to see Trueman at prayer, on his knees at the wicket with eyes averted and hands in supplication. At last Hall set off from the pavilion rails. Fred met the thunderbolt on the front foot with an immaculate drive which went hard along the ground straight to cover. In the stands at the Nursery End there was a buzz of expectation as we prepared for a true contest. At last the unyielding torture of the wooden seats was forgotten in the pleasure of anticipation.

Wes Hall came steaming in from the far distance. This was now in earnest. Again it was lightning fast. Again a good length and again it was met with a resolute front foot drive. Identically immaculate – or was it? It had lifted no more than a foot from the ground and at that height was stingingly and splendidly caught by the MCC ground staff lad at cover. We were stunned. Our entertainment had been brutally curtailed. Trueman out second ball for nought. I suppose I should apologise to Barry Knight and Colin Milburn, who went on to contest the final (Knight was the winner), that I can remember little else of the tournament – a measure of the popular attraction of those two great fast bowlers.

By this time the Trueman arm was starting to get lower. Skill and experience gave him something to fall back on and also gave him some notable successes captaining Yorkshire in the absence of Brian Close. That surprised some people, but the still strong Yorkshire side responded well to the legendary character in their midst, his forthright approach and old fashioned values. In 1965 Fred played his last Test match. A light had gone out – a flame only rekindled since, in England bowling terms, by Willis and Botham on occasions.

Fred was always a performer. He revelled in the spotlight as he held the stage of international cricket, so I suppose it was inevitable that such an entertainer should find his way into broadcasting. But it took a short while for the old pro to shake off some natural reservations. His first arrival in the radio commentary box at the top of the Lord's pavilion was accompanied by the words: 'With a view like this, I feel like a bloody amateur'.

Nearly ten years later, Fred is in his element on Radio Three's

Test Match Special. In command of the situation – as he was in the Yorkshire dressing-room – he is the senior pro to Brian Johnston's amateur captaincy, and between them they account for the bulk of the mail received in the commentary box. Now, as in his playing days, his moods can vary – scowling with indignation one moment at some outrageous piece of cricket, his jaw thrust out defiantly; a sight to make one glad that one is not that unfortunate who was told he would be 'pinned to t'flipping sight-screen' – and the next moment chuckling merrily at some piece of irresistible Johnston humour. Not that Fred is ever behind when jokes are flying around. He is a natural raconteur, greatly in demand for after-dinner speaking and always providing his friends with a new story on each meeting. (Most of them, I have to say, are unlikely to grace the BBC airwaves however liberal we become!) Most listeners – and colleagues – now expect most to hear what has almost become a catch-phrase as he looks, mystified, at the heirs to the game which sustained him for 20 years; 'I simply don't know what's going off!'.

There is one slightly poignant story which arose from Brian Johnston's habit of giving nicknames to one and all. Fred becomes 'Sir Frederick' and when asking his publishers to send him a copy of his latest book, Brian inscribed it 'to Sir Frederick'. The publisher's secretary, seeing the dedication, addressed the package 'Sir Frederick Trueman' and the next day a delighted North Yorkshire postman burst through Fred's front gate, full of congratulations. How Yorkshire would love to celebrate that! Still, the miner's son from Stainton can reflect on a career which made him one of the legendary figures in a game of legends and made him recognisable from Sheffield to Sydney and from Bridgetown to Bradford.

Tom Graveney

FRANK KEATING

I seldom have nightmares. Say a couple a year. But enough to re-establish my stark fear of heights. Extremely scary. I always wake only a split second before I hit the deck – splat! There's a still fevered moment or two for a shaking hand to fumble for the light switch and a smoke. Then, with relief and realisation dawning that I'm both in the land of the living and my pungent pit, I will inhale deeply, smile to myself and, content again, think of . . . Clem Attlee, a former Prime Minister, and George Emmett, a former Gloucestershire bat. And thoughts of George soon turn to recollections of Tom. Ah, Tom. Dear Tom. *Our* Tom.

You need an explanation: in 1946, at the age of eight, I was unaccountably sent the 30 miles from Stonehouse in Gloucestershire to a boarding prep school near Hereford. Now, in spite of his aberration on private education, in all other matters my father, bless him, was as trenchant a socialist as you could ever meet. And you didn't meet many in that true-blue neck of the Randwick Woods unless you bumped into Bert Cole, Ben Parkin, Bill Maddocks or my Uncle John planning the revolution in the Woolpack Inn. Anyway, it so came to pass that, between them, they had won the seat for Labour in the 1945 landslide election. Word of this stunning reverse of the established order seeped even over the county border at about the very same time that I had turned up in Hereford as the most midget, meek and miserable mother's boy even such as Dotheboys had seen. The bigger boys bullied and we namby newts cowered and cringed by day and, at nights, wept and then wet the bed.

Many and varying were the forms of torture. You had done well if you survived a day with only an ear twisted off in the boot room, or a bottom blackened with a scrubbing brush and Cherry Blossom. Most horrendous was 'The Tower', so awful that even the leading sadists only summoned the courage once or twice a year. I

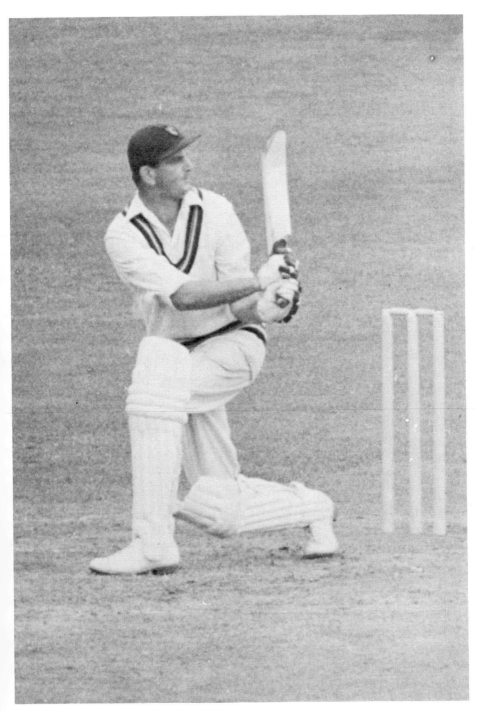

Tom Graveney

heard the dreaded, awful, conspiracy, 'Keating for The Tower tonight; pass it round', whispered through the school on three occasions. The school's church tower was more squat Saxon than tall and fluted Norman. But it was high enough to be absolutely petrifying when you were dangling over its edge held, only by the ankles, by two other boys. The rest of the school would watch the fun from below. I'm still surprised no child ever fell to his death. I am certain it is the reason for my recurring nightmares and my fear of heights. (I can never look out of an aeroplane till it is in the clouds.)

On two occasions I was 'towered' for 'family connections' – that is, every other short-trousered prig in the place was, of course, a Conservative, so when I boasted about my father's and uncle's political affiliations, I did so with my heart in my mouth. I cannot remember exactly why, but I was possibly sent to The Tower when the Labour Party nationalised Steel and when they 'sold out' the Indian Empire to 'the wogs'. I was hung as a martyr for Clem Attlee's great radicalism.

The third time was altogether different. In the midsummer of 1948, the triumphant march of Bradman's Australian cricketers had the English selectors in all sorts of panic. For the third Test match at Old Trafford, out of the blue, they selected two Gloucestershire players. I would have got away with it had the only selection been Jack Crapp, our doughty left-hander who had scored a century against the tourists in the county fixture at Bristol. But the wee sprog, George Emmett, was another matter altogether, for he was chosen to replace Len Hutton, revered both in the school and the land as a national institution. So my one-man Gloucester gloat at Emmett's selection had its comeuppance at once. In a seething fury the word went round, 'Keating for The Tower tonight.' I was hung as a martyr for Georgie Emmett. (When he failed in both innings there were threats that I should be 'done' again.)

Here is the point of these rambling recollections: if George Emmett had not been picked for that one solitary Test match, it is quite possible that the world would never have seen Tom Graveney bat. After Bristol Grammar School and National Service in the Army, young Graveney had seemed to have fluffed his apprenticeship as a Gloucestershire cricketer. At the time of that

Manchester Test match, which began on 8 July, 1948, his 'career' seemed to have ended before it began. On his first-class debut he had made a duck, and followed that with just over 200 runs in 20-odd innings. He was seriously thinking of re-signing for the Army, which he had enjoyed, and taking a PT instructors' course. Certainly he had been demoted to the Gloucester Second XI, and looked unlikely for re-engagement.

Then Crapp and Emmett were selected for England. Graveney was hastily despatched to Bournemouth for the First XI fixture with Hampshire. He made a precocious and calm 47 against the spinners, Knott and Bailey, on a spiteful wicket. In the following match against Somerset at Bristol he scored an undefeated 81. By the time I got home for the holidays, my Stonehouse chums, Peter Beard and Robin Bassett, were filling me in with details of his maiden Test century, against the Combined Services at Gloucester Wagon Works. It had, they said, been amazingly wizard-prang.

The Cheltenham Festival – nine full days of cricket – couldn't come quick enough. Sometimes we'd catch that chippy little chuffer, the 'Railcar', and change at Gloucester. Other mornings would have us in front of the queue outside Woolworth's in Stroud for the Western National double-decker, over the top past Painswick's yews and the Prinknash Pottery. We had our greaseproofed-paper sandwiches, a shilling extra for a bottle of Tizer and a pound of plums, a bat and tennis ball for tea-time, and our autograph books. The first time I saw him, Tom made a silky half-century – all coltish, gangly, upright youthfulness, with a high, twirly, backlift and a stirring, bold, flourishing signature in the follow-through – and he came back to the 'gym', blushing at the applause, and signed my book before he went in to lunch. 'T.W. Graveney', neat, joined-up, surprisingly adult.

Next Easter term, I began to feel less of an outsider at school when Dad sent me a present of my first *Wisden*. Even the bully boys asked, nicely, to borrow it. I would show them the Gloucestershire Notes, and the last sentence about the batting – 'A pleasant feature of the season was the form of a newcomer, T.W. Graveney, a product of Bristol club cricket, who showed graceful right-handed stroke play'.

By Cheltenham that August, the young man was actually leading our parade. That in itself was a triumph. Schoolboy romantics

do not readily forsake their first heroes. And there had been lots of
them about in 'Glorse'. True, Charlie Barnett had gone, off to the
Lancashire League; and, sure, we missed the Chalford autocrat's
hook of nose and stroke; he smacked bumpers, thwack! as if he
was smacking down plaice on the wet slabs outside his fishmon-
gers in 'Zoiren' or 'Chelt'. Then there was the aforementioned
Jack and Georgie. Crapp was the calm and watchful leftie; we were
never in real trouble till he was out. Unperturbable, he would
push his ones and twos to keep the numbers rolling in gentle
rhythms, but then, of a sudden, he would break out and hit the
thing with a clean, wicked ferocity, then lean placid on his sword,
the handle supporting his buttocks like a shooting stick, and he
would cross his arms and legs and wait, serene, while the ball was
retrieved from miles away. 'Good ol' Jack! Give 'em another one,
Jack!' we shouted. But he seldom did it twice in succession. Or
even twice in a session.

Emmett was in direct contrast. A tiny man with a nutbrown face
and whipcord wrists. He had the twinkling feet of an Astaire, and
the same sort of hairstyle. His on-drive singed every blade of grass
between the bowler and mid-wicket. His cap was a very faded blue
because he wore it everywhere – even in bed I bet, we giggled –
and there was always a groan of real sadness when he got himself
out. Emmett, and especially Crapp, I learned many years later,
were the wise and generous mentors and mother-hens to the
young chick Graveney.

In Tom's earliest days, Billy Neale also nursed him in the
middle orders. He was a farmer, from Grace country, down
Thornbury way. He had gone to school, at Cirencester Grammar,
with the county's previous emperor and champion, Wally Hammond, and had always been, they said, the one to understand the
moods and melancholy of that great, smouldering genius. They
would walk together for hours in the orchards of Neale's Bread-
stone Farm, talking of this and that; after which Wally was
refreshed again. Tom's first captain must have been an influence
as well: B.O. Allen was Clifton and Cambridge and once got a
double century against Hampshire; he looked as fierce as our
Latin master and we never dared ask him for an autograph. He
went forth to toss for innings in a brown trilby, like they said
Hammond used to do, and he blew his nose with a whopping,

red-spotted snuff hankie. And like Charlie Barnett, he used to ride to hounds in winter.

There were other tyros, too, with Tom: Milton was to become a dear favourite; the *Yearbook* started calling him 'Clement' and then 'Charlie' before settling, by public demand, on Arthur. He had the soccer player's bow legs – he remains the last 'double' international – and was the most versatile and thrilling fieldsman I ever saw. And Martin Young, suave and smarmy-haired and always beautifully turned out; his bat always looked pine-fresh new. Arrogant, he had South African connections.

Our bowlers would take up another book: we all tried to copy George Lambert's action – he was faster than Lindwall, for sure. His new ball mucker was Colin Scott, who used to work at the Co-op and had great ten-to-two Underwood feet, and occasionally specialised in sixers. There was Sam Cook (whom the Yearbook called 'Cecil' *always*), who was left-arm and reliable and the much-loved apprentice to the very sorcerer himself, our wizard of tweak, Tom Goddard, whose 2,979 career bag of wickets has only been bettered by four others in the whole history of the game. Stumper was Andy Wilson, a tiny tot with massive appeal in every way. He once took ten catches in a match. After all his years keeping to Goddard and Cook, he took bets that he would be the only batsman in the whole land to read Ramadhin's wrong 'un when the West Indies came to Cheltenham in 1950. Both innings Andy shouldered arms to let the little long-sleeved mesmerist's first ball go by outside the off-stump. Both times he was clean bowled. Gloucester were routed that day. Only Graveney made double figures, all blushing uncertainty and middle-of-the-bat, and a man next to me said, 'Our Tom'll be servin' England this side o' twelvemonth'.

And he was. When Denis Compton was injured, Freddie Brown blooded him against the South Africans at Old Trafford in 1951, and on a real sticky he made 15 against Athol Rowan – 'every run full of cultured promise', said John Arlott on the wireless. Tom served England for the next ten years. When George was still King he was taking 175 from the Indians at Bombay; when Lindwall and Miller were still lethal he matched Hutton, stroke for stroke, in a partnership of 168 at Lord's; and a couple of years later he collected a century at Sydney with three

successive boundaries; onwards a summer or two, and his mas-
sively flamboyant 258 nailed down forever the wispy mystique of
Ramadhin and Valentine, after May and Cowdrey had done the
tedious, pad-prod spadework earlier in the month.

Yet while these, and even the shortest innings, were a delight,
word was going about that he lacked the cruel competitive edge to
take a game and an attack by the throat; he was getting out when
the very critical need was just to stay in. He was, horror! playing
Festival cricket instead of Test match cricket. Never the twain
must meet, and he was dropped for, as someone said, 'being
happy only to present his ability, but not to enforce it ruthlessly'.

He had moved from Gloucestershire now. But so had we. And
wherever I was in the world, I daresay I wasn't the only Gloucester
man to sneak a look first at the Worcester scores to see how Tom
had done. For it was soon apparent that there, under the old
Norman shadow that matched the mellow architecture of his
strokes, his batsmanship had actually become even better. It was
still joyous and free of care, but now it was more stable, more
serene, more *certain*. The England selectors, of course, seemed
oblivious to the fact, and though century followed century and
Championship followed Championship, not even the wildest bet-
ting man would have wagered on a recall by England. But at last
they had to. After his four years in the pleasant backwaters of the
shires came an almost tangible rumbling of public demand for
Graveney's Test match place to be restored, following another
woeful England start to the West Indian series of 1966. They
turned to Tom, now in his 40th year.

And at Lord's too! The full-house standing ovation started as he
made his way through the Long Room once again. Hall and
Griffith and Sobers and Gibbs . . . he returned to grandstand
applause after a magnificent 96. 'It's like a dream come true', he
said as he went back up the stairs, eyes moist with tears. In the
next match, at Trent Bridge, England were 13 for 3, Hall's Larry
Holmes and Griffith's Joe Frazier both murderously, cruelly,
hostile. Graveney and Cowdrey alone had the technique and
fearlessness to stand unflinchingly firm. Tom finished with 109,
and many still shake their heads in wonder and insist it must have
been his very best innings.

But there were still more gems in the old man's kitty. A superlative 165 followed at the Oval; then, next summer, a charming 151 comprehensive retrospective – 118 runs against the West Indies. 'Any art gallery in the world would have bought that innings', wrote Henry Blofeld, who was there. He overflowed with fluent strokes and quite outplayed the 1968 Australians, as he did the Pakistanis in the winter, when Karachi saw his last Test match century. When the West Indies rejoined battle next summer he scored 75 in the first Test then, on the free Sunday of the match, played in his own benefit game at Luton. It was against the rules and Lord's banned him for three Tests – in effect forever. But Our Tom of Gloucester had become Worcester's Tom, then England's, then the world's.

As this book is a cricket writers' book, it would be nice to quote the retirement panegyric offered to Graveney after his final Test. It can do more justice than I can to a fine cricketer and a fine man. It was written by one of the very best of writers, J.M. Kilburn, who was for 40 diligent and creative years the correspondent of the *Yorkshire Post*: 'Graveney may have disappointed some cricketers by playing in Graveney's way, but he has adorned cricket. In an age preoccupied with accountancy he has given the game warmth and colour and inspiration beyond the tally of the score-book. He has been of the orchard rather than the forest, blossom susceptible to frost but breathing in the sunshine . . . Taking enjoyment as it came, he has given enjoyment that will warm the winters of memory'.

Yet it might never have happened had George Emmett not been picked for his solitary Test match in the midsummer of 1948. The very same day that Tom was despatched to Bournemouth and I was dangled, head first, from the top of a church tower in Hereford.

Colin Milburn

MATTHEW ENGEL

I ought to remember where I was when the news came, as with Kennedy's assassination or the outbreak of war. But to be honest I have no recollection. It was 23 May, 1969, and I must have been doing my A-Levels. The details of those have been successfully blotted out of my mind since then. The accident in which Colin Milburn lost his left eye and his career must have been thrown out with them.

I do remember that the sinking-in process took longer than usual. Most of us were fooled a little: by inapt comparisons with Pataudi, who played on with his right eye gone; by the wave of hopeful press coverage from the hospitals; by Colin's own quite outstanding bravery. I also remember feeling that if so freakish an injury (why couldn't he just have broken a leg like normal people, for heaven's sake?) could end his career, then it was the saddest possible news for English cricket. Fifteen years on, that thought gnaws at me all the more. Colin Milburn might not have been the greatest cricketer of his generation, but he was, beyond question, the cricketer we could least afford to lose. And we lost him.

I was not and am still not an unbiased observer. Insofar as I ever grew up, I grew up, between bouts of boarding school, in Northampton in the 1960s. This was a bizarre period in English history for many reasons, and one of its minor oddities was that, very briefly, Northampton became the most successful sporting town in the kingdom. In 1965 Northampton Town FC were promoted for their first and only season in the First Division; the rugby club had the best record in England; and the county, after 60 generally disastrous years of first-class cricket, missed the Championship by four miserable points. The cricket team was not only good – we had the best and most exciting young batsman in England.

What's more, he was a friend of mine. Well, more like a friend

Colin Milburn

of a friend actually. But he would recognise me and pass the time
of day and take an interest. I had never spoken to a real cricketer
before, unless he was donating or withholding his autograph,
except for the time Lindsay Hassett burnt my hand with a dog-end
(and he had retired long since so no one was very impressed about
that). It even fell to Colin to coach me at the Easter nets, which he
did without losing his temper. On the basis of this flimsy acquaintance I gave up autograph-hunting as *infra dig* for a friend of the
famous. I realised later that Colin was friends with pretty well
everyone in Northampton. That turned out to be one of his
problems.

Like so many Northamptonshire cricketers, he belonged to the
place only by the curious historical fluke that this insignificant and
apathetic town (with little else to offer except a reasonably quick
train to London) had first-class cricket while County Durham,
which unlike Northamptonshire was somewhere non-cricket
people had heard of, did not. Colin had arrived via Burnopfield
Junior School, Annfield Plain Secondary Modern, Stanley
Grammar and Chester-le-Street in the Durham Senior League (all
faraway places with strange-sounding names but places with
which Northamptonshire kept in touch), because Ken Turner,
the secretary, had offered him ten shillings a week more than
Warwickshire. This transaction achieved slightly more notice
than the acquisition of most young batsmen: Colin had achieved a
sort of public notice as a 17-year-old schoolboy when he made 101
for Durham against the 1959 Indians. He even got a special
mention in the Editor's Notes in the 1960 *Wisden*, amid sections
headed 'Yorkshire's Professional Captain' and 'Welcome South
Africa'! There was also the fact that he was, as *Wisden* put it, 'a
well-built lad' or, to put it another way, fat.

The fat was the first of his trademarks, and the most unconventional. He had always been a tubby boy. In the cold winter of
1963, just as he was becoming established as a county player, he
fought against it furiously and went down from 18 stones to nearer
16. Thereafter, though his weight was a regular talking point
every April and continued to bother selectors – official and arm-
chair ones – of a certain cast of mind, I think it bothered him less. I
often wonder how he might have batted had he slimmed down to
fit the popular perception of what a cricketer should look like. His

batting style was the second and most important of his trademarks, and it must have derived from the first, since so often all his tonnage went into the shot. Yet I don't think there was anything essentially unconventional about his batting. Memory plays odd tricks. I remember the crashing hook, of course; I remember the booming drive, hit most often past a helpless cover point; yet in the mind's eye I can most easily recall that great bulk leaning forward, ever so correctly, to prod away a ball he did not fancy.

The difference between him and everyone else is that he would hit a 50-50 ball, that anyone else would leave or block, and hit it with immense force. Not every time. There is another potent memory: his return to the old and grubby Northampton pavilion, red-faced and as near as he ever got to angry, after a daft nick to first slip or something when in single figures. For us kids, the day moved on to a lower plane. But the good days were electric and if he got past 20, he rarely stopped before 70.

Years later, after the accident, I umpired a village benefit match in which he thumped harmless bowling all over the place for about an hour and I was able to watch at close quarters the visible signs of how he made up his mind what to hit. It occurred to me then that his secret had not been his bulk, nor his technique, nor even the quickness of his poor, damned eyes but the speed of his reflexes. How else could an 18-stone near non-runner come to break the Northamptonshire catching record which he did, in 1964, with 43 catches, almost all at pre-helmet short-leg?

Those reflexes were never infallible. Nor was his judgement, and sometimes the good days were well spaced out. In 1965, five years after he joined Northamptonshire, he went into the final match still short of his 1,000. Gloucestershire were at the County Ground and Northamptonshire needed to win to be Champions. It rained on the first and last days and the fact that Milburn made 152 not out in three and a half hours to get his 1,000 made no difference whatsoever, except to soothe the pain.

That was the beginning of the end of Northampton, Sparta of English sport. The Cobblers had just started their First Division season though it would be almost another three months before they would win a match. The rugby team went through years of mediocrity. And the county still have not been champions yet. But the blazing three-year summer of Colin Milburn's life was just about to start. The following year was the one in which many Championship matches had their first innings restricted to 65 overs. It was one of those early, faltering attempts to enliven the three-day game in response to the success of the Gillette Cup. Colin did not need livening up, but the system suited him very nicely. He began 1966 with two centuries in his first three innings, scored 64 for MCC against West Indies then made 171 at Leicester with Alec Bedser watching. On the Sunday he was in the Test team. Basil D'Oliveira was also in the 12 for the first time (though on that occasion he did not play) and I remember being hurt and puzzled by the 'Hello Dolly' headlines. Milburn did play and soon was being overshadowed by no one.

Nine Test matches – that's all he had time for. He changed four beyond recognition, though it is true that England did not win any of them: a lively but chancy 94 as England went down to that very strong West Indian team, with Sobers, Hall and all, at Old Trafford on his debut; the 126 not out in the next Test at Lord's to save the game (only Colin would save a game by scoring an even-time century); the amazing, fighting 83 at Lord's against the 1968 Australians on a bad wicket; and the final 139 at Karachi the following year, of which more anon.

There would have been time for more but the selectors kept dropping him. Barely a month after the 126 he was gone. He failed in the third Test at Trent Bridge then made 71 for once out at Headingley. I suppose that must have been the game when he was booed for his fielding. I remember it happening somewhere, and only a Headingley crowd could be that crass. At any rate, he was gone the next week along with Cowdrey, the captain, and half his team to make way for the Brian Close era. In that wonderfully vengeful mood that brings out the best in some cricketers, Milburn went to play for Northamptonshire at Clacton and scored 203 not out – a century before lunch, another before tea and a new county first wicket record with Prideaux, who made an occasional contribution (both got nought in the second innings). That year, he was the first to 1,000, scored the fastest century, hit the most sixes and only missed 2,000 because of a broken finger. There was no tour for him to be left out of, so he spent his first happy winter playing for Western Australia.

He had a more moderate year in 1967. He played in two Tests but his best score was 40 at Edgbaston the morning Kunderan had to be given the new ball for India, having taken three wickets in his life. Nonetheless he scored the fastest century of the summer (78 minutes this time, four minutes quicker than the previous year) and was picked to go to the West Indies. When he got there, he started slowly, lost out to Edrich for the first Test and became a spare part.

It was quite clear that a good many influential people did not regard Milburn as a business cricketer. After his Lord's 83 the next year ended in a catch on the deep mid-wicket boundary, one of the selectors commented sourly 'What a way to get out'. He was injured after that and did not return until the Oval-D'Oliveira-Underwood-mopping-up Test, after which he was left out of the South African tour party. Since someone else was also left out, Milburn again found himself overshadowed by D'Oliveira and there are plenty of people around who still believe Milburn's omission was the dafter.

But the curious thing was that Milburn had plenty of detractors in Northampton as well. He had loads of friends. In some cases the same people were in both categories. The County Ground crowds, such as they are, on both the football and cricket sides have long had a fairly well-deserved reputation for sourness. I think the town was much happier when 1965 was over and its teams stopped all this winning nonsense; we could all go back to being happily miserable again. And much of the moaning was at Milburn. There was something not right about all that boozy joviality. Why couldn't he settle down and live and play boringly like you are supposed to do? And poor old Ollie did not seem able to shut them all up by going out and playing one of his really great innings. They always seemed to come somewhere else, somewhere exotic like Lord's or Clacton. Northampton had to be content with some very, very good ones.

Perhaps the greatest of all came that November, even further away. As soon as England left him out of the squad for their non-existent tour to South Africa, Western Australia rang to invite him back. On a fearsomely humid day at the Gabba in Brisbane Milburn went out to open the batting. At lunch he was 61 not out and, rather out of character, complaining; there was so much sweat seeping through his gloves that he could hardly grip the bat. After lunch, the weather cooled a fraction; Milburn went berserk. In the two-hour afternoon session he scored 181. Even Bradman never approached that. He was out the over after tea for 243 and apologised to his team-mates. It may not have registered with everyone in Northampton, but for some of us just hearing about it was something.

He was on a Perth beach with (so the story goes and it is almost certainly true) a couple of birds and a good many beers when, three months later, he got the message that England needed him to reinforce the party for the substitute tour of Pakistan. It is generally held among cricketers that Perth is a better place to be than Dacca and the feeling among the England party at that stage of the tour was, by all accounts, that they should fly out to join Milburn rather than the other way round. But he flew in via one of the most convoluted routes in the history of aviation, and the team summoned up enough energy to give him a guard of honour at the airport and con him into believing that there was no room at the Intercontinental with the other lads and so he would have to stay in a dosshouse next to a swamp.

His very presence had brightened the tour. When they moved to Karachi for the final Test, Milburn was picked and played his last, biggest and probably greatest Test innings, 139 on a dead slow mud pitch at Karachi. As at Northampton, as with the England selectors, he was not wholly appreciated – the crowd were too busy rioting to take much interest. But, as the game was abandoned after the gates were smashed by the crowd, it was generally agreed that whatever else had gone wrong for English cricket that winter – and pretty well everything had – at least Milburn had now emerged as a genuine Test batsman, and not just a slogger.

The summer of 1969 marked the start of the Sunday League which, genuine Test batsman or not, might have been designed for Milburn's personal use. He began the season with 158 against Leicestershire and played his part in a Northamptonshire win over the West Indies. His selection for the first Test was now not even a matter for discussion. And then it happened.

I was a schoolboy still and cannot be certain that all the smiling pictures were not just a front for the camera. But the sister-in-charge said his manner never changed in his 11 days in hospital, the hospital management committee singled him out in their annual report ('his infectious good humour and indomitable spirit raised morale throughout the hospital') and in the years since I have still not glimpsed whatever sadness lurks behind the mask.

Four years later, when he made his brief and abortive come-back, I was just starting to make my way as a cricket writer in Northampton and was close enough to pick up the jealousy among some of the Northamptonshire players who thought he should not be playing. The come-back did not fail by much – with his little bit of medium pace bowling, he was almost good enough to play county cricket – but the glory had departed and he knew it.

There is a curious historical parallel. After the last match of the 1936 season the two Northamptonshire openers, A.H. Bakewell and R.P. Northway, were returning by car from Chesterfield. Bakewell had scored 241 not out and had almost taken Northamptonshire, the bottom county, to victory over Derbyshire, the top county. Bakewell had played six Tests, three fewer than Milburn. The car crashed, Northway was killed, and Bakewell, who hovered near death for several days, never played again. Thereafter he lived a shadowed and apparently sad life. Colin Milburn spent a good deal of the time (too much, said all Northampton) after his accident in his old corner spot at the bar of the Abingdon Park Hotel, always with a happy group, in shadow, but obviously not in sadness. Then, quietly and suddenly, he left Northampton and returned to County Durham. There are still booze and birds but no marriage and, for a man past 40, no obvious purpose. He has been doing this and that. He still comes to the odd London do. He still smiles. We still chat.

He might yet find his *métier* on the radio. His occasional commentaries have been shrewd and funny and generous, because he does not believe no one else can play. Please may he find his way. His indomitable spirit did not only raise morale at the hospital; it lit up my youth.

Jim Parks

ALAN ROSS

'Sussex may or may not win a match,' Neville Cardus once wrote, 'but I have never watched Sussex with my eyes on the score-board, calculating results. I have watched with the eyes and affection of a lover of the game who knows a Sussex cricketer at sight, a cricketer who plays the game with all his heart and to his heart's content.' Such a sentiment, coming from a Lancastrian, is worth preserving, but it is doubtful whether there are many batsmen in the long history of Sussex entertainers to whom it applies more accurately than J.M. Parks. There were Ranji and Duleep, of course; Ted Bowley and Alan Melville, Hugh Bartlett and George Cox, cricketers of elegance and dash in the decades before the war, but since 1945, if one had to name the Sussex batsman who has consistently given more pleasure than any other, it could only be Jim Parks.

The word 'pleasure' is the operative one. I cannot recall offhand a 'great' innings by Jim, in the graver sense that I can remember 'great' innings played by Leonard Hutton and Tom Graveney, by Peter May and Colin Cowdrey, by Frank Worrell and Everton Weekes, by Ted Dexter and Gary Sobers and Graeme Pollock among others. In any case, I must have seen only a fraction of the innings Jim Parks has played. But what was unmistakable – and this was usually the case, in slightly lesser degree, for England as for Sussex – was the manner in which he came to the wicket, the apparent light-heartedness he brought even to the grimmest of situations. There was an almost immediate lessening of tension, itself dispersed further by the flashing cover drives with which he habitually announced himself.

It was rumoured by some that, at the highest level, Jim was a fair-weather cricketer, but I don't think there is much evidence for this. He might, by scoring freely while others had struggled, give an impression that he had no heart for fight, but he was by

Jim Parks

nature a batsman of airs and graces, and who is to say that a beautiful stroke made with a smile is less effective than a forward prod made with a face as miserable as sin? If batsmen were to be penalised for the runs they failed to score off balls they should have scored from, then Jim Parks would stand much higher in the list than some of greater renown. He had a decent appetite for runs, but never a greed for them at any price.

It would be out of the question for me to have a real cricketing hero outside Sussex. From the day I arrived from India at the age of seven Sussex became my home, and its cricket my passion. Brought up by the Rector of Ardingly as one of Kipling's 'stranger's children' while my parents were in India, the first county cricket I ever saw was at Hove in 1933. Sussex was captained then by R.G.S. Scott, who succeeded Duleep, and was replaced in his turn by the graceful Alan Melville. Sussex were runners-up in the Championship under each of them in successive seasons. Ted Bowley and Maurice Tate were coming to the end of their careers, but John and James Langridge, J.H. and Harry Parks, Bert Wensley, 'Tich' Cornford and Tommy Cook were present for most of the time. There was not much in the way of bowling – Jim Langridge's patient left-arm spin and Jim Parks senior's gentle in-dippers to support Jim Cornford and the aging Tate – but by the end of the decade Hugh Bartlett had arrived to tear attacks to pieces, George Cox was reaching his inventive peak, Charlie Oakes was languidly promising what he never quite bothered to achieve, and Jack Nye was picking up wickets after a run-up that reached to the sight-screen.

In the holidays, when Sussex were playing away, there was cricket at Haywards Heath, home of the Parks brothers, and of Jim's son Jim, born in 1931. In the Rectory garden at Ardingly, games, following the same hours as county matches, were played day in, day out, by myself and the other 'stranger's children' boarded there. Then came the war, and afterwards Sussex were not, and could hardly have been expected to be, the same. Jim and John Langridge were still going strong, and, in exotic bursts, George Cox, too. Bartlett was a shadow of his pre-war self and there were no aggressive bowlers at all. In the first season of peace Sussex finished bottom. It was not until the arrival, in the early 1950s, of Ian Thomson and Robin Marlar that the bowling picked up enough to give a gradually blossoming batting side any chance of winning matches.

In 1953, Sussex, under David Sheppard, with George Cox like a wise old owl at his shoulder, finished second yet again. It was the best they were to manage for nearly 30 years, and they managed it, as much as anything, by making large scores in the fourth innings against the clock.

It was in 1953 that I became cricket correspondent of *The Observer* and as much as was decently possible I tried to make duty coincide with pleasure over the next 20 years. That I was able to do so with some justification was due to the presence in the Sussex side of Jim Parks, Alan Oakman, Ted Dexter and John Snow, and on occasions David Sheppard, Hubert Doggart and 'Tiger' Pataudi. If Sussex still lacked the all-round strength to challenge in the Championship during this time, they were the first county to make a mark on one-day cricket, winning the Gillette Cup in its first two years. No one was more exciting to watch in this competition than Jim. I have a weakness for batsmen who like to hit the ball over the field as well as through it and Jim's skimming drives in the arc between mid-on and cover were something to behold.

In 1937 Jim's father, J.H., had achieved the unique double of 3,003 runs and 103 wickets, Jim Langridge scoring 2,082 runs and taking 101 wickets in the same season. I fancy it was that summer when I first set eyes on 'old' Jim's son, a frail-looking fair-haired boy of six standing to one side while his father tried to explain the flow of runs pouring from his bat. In that magical summer J.H. hit 11 hundreds, hooking and cutting with sudden perfection of timing. With his red cheeks and glistening black hair, head set deep into his shoulders, he was like a little robin, bird-like and pecking in all his movements. The family resemblance in feature, if not in colouring, remains.

The next time I became aware of young Jim was in 1950 when I saw him at at Lord's against Middlesex. I had heard rumours of this promising leg-spinner and spectacular cover point, who had been given a game or two for the county at the end of the previous season, and naturally everyone hoped for another Parks to carry on the county's family tradition. I'm not sure what the state of the match was when Jim, then 19 years old, came in. I do remember that David Sheppard was batting at the other end and looking a

shade cumbersome against the spin of Jim Sims and Freddie
Titmus. Suddenly, bowling that had been tying experienced
batsmen up in knots was cut, glanced and driven all over the place.
Here was a boy who came down the pitch to scotch the spin and
who seemed to have, as well as an instinctive appreciation of
length, technical resource and daring. I don't think Jim can have
batted for more than about 40 minutes and he made only 36, but it
was apparent beyond doubt that he was a batsman of immense
talent. He looked certain to develop into not just a good, but – less
common – an exciting player. Not long afterwards, at Gillingham,
he made his first hundred for the county against a Kent attack that
included Doug Wright.

There was no looking back after that, though there were the
inevitable ups and downs. National Service in the RAF claimed
him during the winter, and the next summer he made only occasional appearances for Sussex, the Combined Services, where his
colleagues included Trueman, Illingworth, Moss and Titmus,
usually claiming him. He did, however, make one remarkable
appearance for Sussex, at Tunbridge Wells, and I was there to see
it. With James Langridge, now 45 and an almost exact contemporary of his father's, he put on 294 for the third wicket, Jim's
own share being an exuberant 188.

It was not in Jim Langridge's nature to hurry over anything,
especially as he grew older and heavier. He was one of the most
effortless and relaxed cricketers that ever reached the top, a man
who batted and bowled to a lazy inner music. But that day he
would have been run off his feet if Parks' drives had not gone
whistling so frequently into the rhododendrons. There was something immensely touching about that partnership, almost the last
embrace, as it were, between two generations. Soon the Lan-
gridges had departed and then George Cox, the last to have played
with young Jim's father. But watching these two together was
bearing witness to the Sussex torch being handed down, if not
quite from father to son, then from family to family.

A county cap soon followed, and then a marvellous hundred at
The Oval against Surrey's all-star attack. With his return in 1952
to the Sussex side, however, the real business of Jim Parks' career
began. As often as not, at least for the first few years, John
Langridge or George Cox were watching critically at the other

end, but after that it was David Sheppard, Ken Suttle or Alan Oakman, even for a while, Richard Langridge, son of James.

The ten years between 1955 and 1965, when Ted Dexter departed, were wonderful years for watching Sussex bat. I don't suppose Jim Parks ever hit the ball quite as hard as Ted, but he made the game look easier and he scored just as fast. He was, I believe, the more polished batsman of the two, though less commanding and destructive than Dexter at his best. He and Suttle ran like hares between the wickets and there seemed a great friendliness and good nature, as well as chattering, about Sussex, whether batting or in the field.

Jim had been playing cricket for the best part of ten years before the question of keeping wicket arose. It was not an area in which Sussex had been particularly distinguished during that time, but it was an injury to the regular wicket-keeper, Rupert Webb, in the late summer of 1958, that changed the course of Parks' career. He stepped in on a temporary basis and was so successful that he took over full-time in 1959, heading the list of English wicket-keepers with 86 catches and seven stumpings. An efficient long-stop at the start of that season, he was stylish and professional by the end of it, scarcely missing a chance. Because he began the job late, and in the way he did, there were always those ready to decry Parks' wicket-keeping, but he kept for England in over 40 Tests, was often picked in wicket-keeping merit over John Murray and only once, towards the end, when in Australia he missed a crucial stumping off Bob Barber, cost his side anything.

It is unlikely, I suppose, that Jim would have played in anything like as many Tests had it not been for his extraordinary progress during and after that first season of wicket-keeping. He had, it is true, played one Test as a batsman, as far back as 1954 against Pakistan, but thereafter he had to compete with May, Cowdrey, Graveney, Barrington, Dexter and M.J.K. Smith, among others. But now his luck turned. He was coaching in Trinidad when a series of injuries and illnesses caused Walter Robins, the MCC manager, to send for Jim. He made 186 in his first innings and was eventually preferred to the two official wicket-keepers, Swetman and Andrew, for the crucial fifth Test. Parks made 43 and 101 not out, batting in uncharacteristically dogged fashion, and England held their 1-0 lead to win the series.

Jim was still regarded, in Test terms, as a reserve wicket-keeper, but in 1963 another chance came his way. He played in all five Tests against Australia in England in 1964; in South Africa the following winter he added 206 for the sixth wicket with Ken Barrington in the Durban Test, scoring 108 not out; and in Australia in 1965-66 he made scores of 52, 71, 13, 49, 16 and 89, usually batting at number seven. In addition there were whole series against India, West Indies and New Zealand, altogether 46 Test appearances, his 114 Test dismissals putting him third among English wicket-keepers to Knott and Evans. Considering he was 28 before he kept wicket seriously, it was not bad going.

But figures were never what Jim Parks' cricket was about. He brought to the game a rare sense of delight, an elegance of touch and movement that rarely failed to lift the spirits. His Test innings, apart from his two centuries, were usually beautiful cameos, eye-catching affairs that often were over too soon. For Sussex, however, batting number four, he was the leading scorer for 20 years, only John Langridge scoring more runs in the history of the county.

Sussex cricket is continuity: Ranji to Duleep, George Cox to George Cox, Fred Tate to Maurice Tate, James and John Langridge to Richard Langridge, J.H. Parks and Harry Parks to J.M. Parks, S.C. Griffith to M.G. Griffith, the Gilligan brothers, the Busses and the Oakeses. There will soon be more to come, no doubt, from the Lenhams amongst others, for it is unthinkable that there should be a Sussex side without a family connection.

In the meantime, if I want to think of something truly happy, it is of a blue day at Hove, the sea-fret giving way to sea-dazzle, the hock on ice, and Jim Parks coming out to bat. In store, there will be that familiar repertoire of cover drives, lofted hits over mid-off and extra, pulls into the pavilion, and late cuts running down towards the sea. More than anything there will be the sense of adventure, the absence of restraint, that go to make an occasion.

I don't quite know why Jim did not work out as a captain, though Sussex were not easy to captain in the late 1960s and he received little support from colleagues or Committee, and in any case it does not matter. He gave immense pleasure and it was players like Jim whom Neville Cardus had in mind when he wrote what I quoted at the start of this piece.

Ken Barrington

CHRISTOPHER MARTIN-JENKINS

It seems impossible that it is now three years since Ken Barrington died. He had a vitality which was irresistible and it hangs in the memory like a good tune.

I first saw him batting for Surrey in 1955 when I was only ten and making my first visit to The Oval. Ken was already 25 and only now fully establishing himself as a first-class cricketer after eight years on the staff, one of the longest apprenticeships of any great player. But this, of course, was one of the strongest staffs any county ever had, and Ken had been away for years on National Service duty. The discipline learned then, and no doubt already imparted at home in Reading by his father, a regular soldier, served him well through both the difficult first phase of his career and the years of success which followed.

You could, indeed, sense the discipline in his deportment on the field. Everything about him was neat and compact. My memory of that first innings I saw him play for Surrey is a hotchpotch of visual impressions: the black, crinkly hair, bare to the sun as in England it almost always was; an air of purposefulness and bustle; a propensity to chatter and chuckle between overs, with his batting partner (I think for much of that day it was little Bernie Constable) or with opposing fielders; a number of firm drives, through extra cover or wide of mid-on; and one shot in particular, a very late cut, the Stuart Surridge bat coming firmly down on to the ball as it drew level with the off-stump, sending the ball scudding down to where my brother and I sat entranced, between the pavilion and the gas-holders. For some reason that shot, the dark red ball bobbling rapidly over the green turf towards us, and the words of an old Oval pensioner, 'All the way, all the way', remain vividly in my mind.

The match was in August, after Ken Barrington had made his first appearance for England, against South Africa. Looking back

Ken Barrington

this must have been why at this stage he had a special interest for a young spectator. The man who was to score 6,806 runs for England at an average of 58; who was to hit 20 hundreds in 82 Tests; and who was to become the most reliable middle-order batsman of his time started for England at Trent Bridge by lasting three balls – caught by John Waite off the fair-haired, medium-fast Eddie Fuller. Captained for the first time by Peter May, England won by an innings. At Lord's in the second Test he made 34 in the first innings, top score on a lively wicket, choosing to hook Heine and Adcock and having some luck; and 18 in the second. He did not play for his country again for four years. Incidentally, did England ever go through a home season with three more unlikely combinations of opening batsmen than in that 1955 season? Graveney and Kenyon, followed by Bailey and Lowson and Ikin and Close: two all-rounders, one middle-order batsman and three specialist openers who never quite made it at the highest level.

The mid-50s, despite being highly successful for England, saw a good deal of chopping and changing by the selectors amongst the batsmen, although it was a golden era for bowlers – Trueman, Statham, Tyson, Bedser, Bailey, Laker, Lock, Wardle – all indisputably world class in their different ways. But only in 1959 when Ken Barrington returned to provide the ballast which enabled the sails of May and Cowdrey – and, all too fitfully at this time of Graveney and the emerging Dexter – to billow out in all their glory, did the good ship England lay firm claim to the blue Riband.

It is worth considering whether England would have been as humiliated as they were the winter before Barrington re-established himself as a Test player if he had been to Australia with Peter May. In theory England were not short of batsmen of class or determination on that trip. But just think how Barrington played in the West Indies the following winter – hundreds in the first two Tests – and in Australia on his first visit in 1962-63, when his last four Test innings were 63, 132 not out, 101 and 94; followed by 126, 76, 47 and 45 in three Tests against New Zealand. Might not he have withstood the menace by Meckiff for longer than some of those who went?

This was the wonderful thing about the mature Ken Barrington: his consistency. Wally Grout's famous observation that he

seemed to walk out to bat with a Union Jack trailing behind him
was apt enough, for Ken was a tremendous patriot and, well as he
often batted for Surrey, he was always at his best for England,
when he literally believed himself to be fighting for his country.
But there is an element of selfishness in every cricketer, and in the
years between his premature elevation to Test status and his
return in 1959, Ken Barrington worked out a batting philosophy
which, though it often bored spectators and invoked official dis-
pleasure, notably when he was dropped for scoring too slow and
'selfish' a century against New Zealand in 1965, nevertheless
served him and his country well. In his early days in the Surrey
Second XI he had been a batsman with a full array of strokes, hit
with tremendous power borne of natural timing and the square-
shouldered strength which he carried below that craggy chin and
almost de Bergeracian nose. He became frugal with all the strokes
which lay within his power, at least until he was fully established
at the crease. But often, after reaching 100 (and for a time he
acquired a habit of doing so with a six, as a sort of penance for the
fastidious care which had gone into the first 94 runs) he would
release the pent-up tension and hours of single-minded concentration in a glorious array of drives, hooks and square-cuts.

There were days when he was so out of form that he really would
look a strokeless, boring player, days when, as he would have said,
he 'couldn't hit the skin off a rice pudding'. But there were many
others when one felt that, even when he was allowing himself to
loosen the reins and score freely, there was a marvellous security
about his batting. The defence was solid and uncomplicated,
based more on the back foot against fast bowling than that of many
English players, and always resolutely in line against the quick
stuff, even though he often looked discomforted by the short
lifters of which Hall and Griffith in particular often gave him more
than his share. In attack, like all top-class players, he was prolific
between mid-wicket and mid-on and, despite the open stance
which he developed in mid-career, his off-side strokes were played
with text-book positioning and the precision of a drill sergeant.
For all his emphasis on defence there was a crisp decisiveness
about the attacking strokes and, against the spinners, a willingness to use his feet to get to the pitch of the ball and lift it over the
bowler or to mid-off or mid-on.

It was somehow cruelly appropriate that the heart attack which ended his career, and the one which ended his life, should both have been suffered overseas. He was destined to spend much of his time playing on foreign fields and it was on the overseas tours that English cricket supporters often had most cause to be grateful for his solid consistency as England's number three or four. Under a burning sun before an alien crowd Barrington the batsman was in his element. And so he was, too, when the day's work was done, because it was then that the humorist in him was at its most valuable for the morale of his team.

Ken, in fact, was four comedians in one: a visual comic who could exploit something unusual on the field and play on it to the crowd's amusement; a natural mimic who could impersonate some of the characters in the game; a quick wit when it came to dressing-room repartee; and, perhaps above all, an unconsciously funny man who spread great mirth by getting well-known phrases or proverbs slightly wrong. He would talk, for example, of England 'hanging on by their eyelashes' or a bird in the hand being worth 'two in the basket'. Tony Greig's hundred at Calcutta in 1977 was a 'great innings in any cup of tea' and he assured a gathering of dignitaries in Sri Lanka that they hadn't 'fallen down on any failings'.

Ken's enthusiasm and optimism allied to a willingness to help everyone connected with that particular MCC tour of India did much to help not just the team but the press too. Everyone was greeted with the same cheery grin, jaw thrust out in friendship. But behind the smiles and jokes was a restless, worrying mind. As a player he had smoked too much and had often needed to resort to sleeping pills to stop him from fretting all night about the challenge facing him the next day. As a manager the responsibilities facing him were more varied and sometimes less easy to solve. These things contributed to his shockingly early death in Barbados in 1981. A young and outplayed England team was shattered by the passing of the man they called 'The Colonel'.

Ken was a great batsman, a valuable and under-used leg-spin bowler and a fine fielder with a strong throw and quick reflexes in the slips. He was also one of the most conscientious, dogged and honest-to-goodness characters who ever pulled on an England sweater. And no one ever did so with greater pride.

Gary Sobers

TONY COZIER

When I was at school in the mid-1950s, with what were then the British West Indies gradually moving from three centuries of European colonialism towards independence, our history teacher asked us to write an essay on the most influential figures in that development. Having set the subject, he quickly added: 'And I don't mean the three Ws or Ramadhin and Valentine!'. It was a light-hearted quip to boys who, at the time, were glorying in the deeds of Clyde Walcott, Everton Weekes and Frank Worrell; of 'those two little pals of mine' Sonny Ramadhin and Valentine; and of the many others who were combining to make the West Indies cricket team one of the strongest in the game. Yet the role of our sportsmen, and more especially our cricketers, in the moulding of a West Indian identity and self-confidence cannot be underestimated.

By its very nature, the 'colonial experience', as the university analysts now like to refer to it, left us devoid of our own heroes. Our peoples came by various routes for various reasons to these islands; from Europe, from Africa, from India, and, through a careful process of education, came to regard Britain as the Mother Country, to take English as the common language, to learn the history of Britain and the British. We also learned to play cricket and, through the game, found a means of demonstrating to the world our potential for excellence long before political independence became a reality. What is more, we were represented, from the earliest days, as the West Indies, so that, through cricket more than anything else, we came to see ourselves as West Indians, rather than Jamaicans or Barbadians or Trinidadians or any of the several nationalities which have proliferated of late because of the divisiveness of insular politics.

Almost 80 years after the first West Indies cricket team ventured across the Atlantic on its first tour of England, our cricket

Gary Sobers

remains the main unifying force of the people of the former British colonies in the Caribbean, people now divided into several mini-nations, suspicious of each other in matters of politics and finance.

No two West Indians I know are held in higher esteem by their people than the two knights, Sir Frank Worrell and Sir Garfield Sobers, for no two West Indians did more to enhance the prestige of our cricket than they. It was Worrell, born and bred in Barbados, later to reside in Jamaica where he was appointed to the Senate, and then in Trinidad where he became an administrator at the University of the West Indies, who brought his players together into a true team, emphasising their West Indianness and leading the strongest combination we have ever had. After his early death at the age of 42 there might have been a vacuum in West Indies cricket, a reversal of his commitment to unity, had not he been succeeded by Sobers. By then, Sobers had already established himself, beyond doubt, as the finest cricketer of his generation, arguably of any generation. As captain, he embellished that reputation and the reputation of West Indian cricket, not, let it be admitted, by his tactical reading of the game, but by his approach to and deep affection for it. In whatever Sobers did, he gave the distinct impression that the game was to be enjoyed, its image glorified, never sullied.

It was an attitude which he developed as a boy, barefooted and in short trousers, perpetually playing any form of cricket that was available in the Bayland district just outside Bridgetown. The Sobers family was poor by most standards and had lost its bread-winner, Gary's seaman father, when a German torpedo sunk the merchant ship on which he was serving. The young Sobers, a left-hander with such natural gifts that anyone seeing him even briefly realised he had been placed on this earth for the clear purpose of playing cricket, was soon attracting attention. Despite his age, then 14, and his size, a country team snatched him away from the Bayland club, which had been reluctant to use him in senior games. The next step was into the Barbados Cricket Association Division One Championship where the Test players did their stuff, but it took the initiative of the Assistant Commissioner of Police, a former Barbados captain, Wilfred Farmer, to spot the potential of the young Sobers and to shoot him straight into the band so that he could play for the force.

So started one of the most magnificent careers the great game has known, and those of us who lived through it can count ourselves fortunate. As a West Indian, and a close personal friend of Sobers, I am probably biased but I do not expect to see again anyone who can make this intricate and, for most of us, difficult game appear so ridiculously easy.

The West Indies were in Perth for the opening of the 1868-69 tour of Australia – a disastrous tour as it turned out – when Sobers roused himself from half-slumber in the players' area to go out to bat. The West Indians were in some trouble at the time, just over 100 for 4 with Roy Fredericks, having been hit on the head by Graham McKenzie, nursing a pounding head on the physio's couch in the dressing-room. As always, the WACA pitch was lightning fast and bouncy and, in addition to McKenzie, the state side included Laurie Mayne, another Australian fast bowler, the left-handed Sam Gannon, young and distinctly sharp, and the wily old Tony Lock in their attack. As Sobers strode in, the young wicket-keeper Michael Findlay excused himself from a net session to have a look at his captain in action. Being from St Vincent, where little first-class cricket was played at the time, he had never seen the great man bat. What he saw was termed 'incredible' by *Wisden*, a record never prone to exaggeration. In under two hours, Sobers flayed the bowling – the faster it came, the harder it went – hitting 132 with 25 fours on what, at the time, was the largest outfield in the first-class game. I'll never forget that innings, nor will I ever forget Michael Findlay at the dinner table at the Perth Travelodge that night, full of excitement and awe of the first innings he had ever seen Sobers play.

There were, of course, so many other performances of like quality, many made when his team was in dire trouble. His eyesight, his reflexes, his co-ordination had to be exceptional but, to me, there was nothing as fascinating about Sobers as his self-confidence. I never saw him tense before a big match, never worried about the conditions or his own form. Quite the contrary, he appeared to take all cricket as he took his boyhood games in the Bayland. He would often say, openly, that he felt good and that he would make runs the next day. He would invariably be right.

We were, for instance, in Adelaide for the fourth Test of that same 1968-69 series in Australia when I received news of the birth

of our first child, a boy. Needless to say, this was a cause for
celebration and I packed the motel refrigerator with adequate
supplies in anticipation of being joined by members of the team
when they got back from an official reception. However, the Test
was the next day, it was a crucial one (we were 2-1 down) and
everyone was keen to have an early night. Except Gary. He knew
me, and my wife, well and insisted that we should not allow a Test
to spoil the occasion. He was familiar with Adelaide after years of
playing for South Australia and, with a mutual Barbadian friend,
Dr Rudi Webster (ex-Warwickshire, then, as now, resident in
Australia) we headed out. Guiltily, I tried to persuade Gary, in the
wee hours of the morning, that enough was enough, but he would
have none of it. 'Look, I'm feeling good. Don't worry about me',
he responded. I needn't have worried. Next day, he got a brilliant
110 in just over two hours.

   It was the type of confidence I saw repeated time and again, and
it transmitted itself to his partners. In his time as captain, Sobers
was repeatedly criticised for batting too low in the order at number
six, yet, as he would point out, he seldom ran out of partners and
often pulled the team round with help from a tail-ender. There is
no better way to judge the character of a sportsman than to assess
him in a crisis. In such situations, Sobers was at his best. At
Lord's, in 1966, when the West Indies were seemingly down and
out just before lunch on the fourth day, a mere nine runs in their
second innings with five wickets down, his cousin, David Holford
– in only his second Test – joined him. Not once demeaning his
inexperienced partner by shielding him from the strike, Sobers
led by example: both scored centuries, their sixth wicket stand
was a record 276 unbroken and the match was not only saved but
very nearly won.

   At Sabina Park, in 1968, Sobers was at the wicket when the
West Indies position appeared so desperate that the crowd could
not contain its disappointment and halted play by throwing bot-
tles in protest at what they thought to be a dubious decision.
Following on, the West Indies had half their wickets down at the
time and were still behind on a wickedly unpredictable pitch. Yet
Sobers was still in and, as at Lord's almost two years earlier, he
finished with an unbeaten century and the West Indies not only
saved, but almost won, the match.

On each occasion, the Sobers confidence had been displayed in a declaration which bordered on arrogance. At Lord's, he closed with five wickets down and challenged England to score 284 in four hours. They were 67 for 4 and facing defeat before Graveney, back in the side after an absence of three years, and Colin Milburn, big and belligerent with a century in only his second Test, foiled Sobers' bid. At Sabina, England had protested at the crowd interruption, thinking at the time that the hour and a quarter lost would have been to their advantage. The West Indies Board agreed to make up the time on an unscheduled sixth day but, in the end, England were the ones desperately hanging on, at 68 for 8.

It was inevitable that one day such bravado would backfire on Sobers, and it did in the very next Test of that 1968 series at the Queen's Park Oval in Port-of-Spain. A high-scoring match was drawing to a boring conclusion on the final day with England delivering 22 overs in the two hours before lunch. Exasperated by the stalemate in the match and the series to date, Sobers suddenly surprised all and sundry by declaring and setting England 215 to win in the final two and three-quarter hours. This proved a miscalculation – England, paced by Boycott and skipper Colin Cowdrey, got the runs, to the consternation of a West Indian public which does not take kindly to losing at the best of times, far less in such a manner. Sobers' earlier, successful declarations were forgotten, effigies of the captain were hung in Port-of-Spain's Independence Square and Sobers was made to realise that this was an indiscretion for which he would never be forgiven.

Yet he took the frenzied criticism stoically and steeled himself to make amends by levelling the series in the final Test in Georgetown. He himself could have done no more in his attempt to pay off his debt. He scored 152 and 95 not out, taking three wickets in each innings and bowling 68 overs in all. Yet, at the end, England held out with nine wickets down. Perhaps, with a little more sympathetic umpiring, Sobers might have got the victory he yearned for. But he made no mention afterwards of his acute disappointment and was above trying to pass the buck to the umpires or anyone else.

In an era when umpires and officials are so frequently badgered by players and when captains are inclined to make public pronouncements on decisions which have not gone in their favour,

the example of Sobers – and, indeed, that of Worrell – appears to
have been forgotten. Sadly, Worrell's influential presence was lost
with his sudden death. It is a matter of equal regret that Sobers, a
true West Indian hero, has been lost to West Indian cricket and
that he has been passing on his knowledge and experience to
Australians and Sri Lankans in recent times. It is to be hoped that
his absence from the Caribbean is only temporary. We can ill
afford to lose one of our heroes. We have so few of them.

John Snow

ALAN LEE

Hove, 1965: bad light stopped play. The card schools and custom-
ary banter doubtless began in the Sussex dressing-room, but my
hero appeared at the top of the pavilion steps, located a friend and
sat down on one of those distinctive park-bench seats to chat. Now
was the moment for the intrepid autograph-hunter to strike.
Gathering the courage I had hitherto hidden from all humanity
and school-chums alike, I darted up the steps, head down,
plastic-bound book outstretched. Somehow I expected a tetchy
rebuff but it failed to transpire. While I looked around me in
feverish expectation of some giant 'jobsworth' barging along to
give me a justly jostling exit, the book was signed with a flourish. I
departed with stuttered thanks to view my prize, and from that
moment on, John Snow was even more of a hero than before.

It might not have looked like it, a year or so ago, to fellow
inmates of the Test match press boxes. There we were, Snowy and
I, colleagues in tabloid cricket-writing, arguing first over which
angle each of us should take and then which of us should be first to
use the Associated Newspapers 'phone. He had not fallen as a
hero; it was much more pleasant than that – he had become a
workmate, a friend. Not many, I guess, can say that of their
childhood idol.

I was 11 years old in that summer of 1965. My thoughts were
full of the step up from junior to grammar school, of the bruises on
my thumb from trying to hold a stinging catch off the sports
master in the end-of-term cricket game, of fanciful romances and
fear of water. And, as important and prominent as any other
subject, of an ambition to bowl fast. John Snow was fast – I knew
that much from the papers and the television. That day at Hove,
however, was my first chance to see him in person, and I had to
confess I was suitably impressed. He was, after all, everything that
a schoolboy cricket dreamer would have liked to be: tall, lean,

John Snow

dark, undeniably handsome, undemonstratively athletic and with
a streak of aggression to scare the weak at heart. I wanted to be like
that. In my realistic moments I knew it was not an odds-on bet,
but what the hell? I was 11, and a dreamer.

I had no local rights to being a Sussex follower. Born in Middlesex and brought up in Hertfordshire, I still don't quite know
how my affinity developed, except that, in Ted Dexter, Jim Parks
and Snow himself, Sussex had the three cricketers I most admired
during that first stage of my love-affair with the game. They were
the county whose scores I scoured first when the morning paper
flopped on to our doormat in commuter country. They were the
county I continually pestered my parents into taking me to see,
until finally they agreed. They were the county I cheered and cried
tears of joy over, as they dominated the early years of the Gillette
Cup under 'Lord Ted'.

John Augustine Snow, born during the ravaging years of the
Second World War in the Worcestershire countryside, had
emerged as a character by then. Emerged from a boyhood spent,
in his own words, 'hawk-like, wheeling and swooping on the
innocent pleasures of the countryside'. Fishing, bird's-nesting,
scrumping, even the hunting of snakes and the training of jack-
daws – these were the pursuits of Snow in his youth. But, as both
grandfather and father were members of the clergy, he also sang in
the church choir. If this side of him was not entirely misleading,
for he has always possessed a peaceful, thought-provoking element, then neither did it dominate. 'I did my fair share of fighting
to find an outlet for my aggressive streak', he recalls, especially
bringing to mind a particular scrap in the school porch. 'I caught
my opponent with a beautiful punch. It ended the fight, but
unfortunately he went back through the door and landed at the
headmaster's feet. I ended by losing out to the cane.'

A good net, this, for the scraps to come on Test grounds around
the world, in which Snow developed the well-deserved reputation
of being the most hostile weapon to come out of England since
Trueman at his peak. His career, like Trueman's before him, was
at times caught in such turbulent waters it almost overturned
completely, for Snow the cricketer could be an uncompromising
character both on and off the field. He never had a great deal of
time for pedantic regulations designed to promote bureaucracy

rather than aid players; neither did he make any secret of his views. Inevitably, then, there were clashes with authority – as the cliché has it – scattered untidily among the heroic deeds for which I prefer to remember him.

Casting back now, it seems a wicked scandal that he played only 49 Tests. After all, David Gower passed that figure in less than five years; Snow, at least Gower's equal if in a different department, represented his country over 12 English summers from 1965 to 1976 and, extraordinary to relate, went on only three tours. Some absences, admittedly, were of his own choice: he elected not to tour Pakistan and India in the winter of 1972-73, for instance, because on his previous trip to the former country in 1969 he had contracted a touch of dysentry, the effects of which lingered for almost a year. 'I thought hard and long before telling Alec Bedser I would not be available . . . I decided that I was not going to expose myself to the danger of catching it again.'

All that was in the future when I first set eyes on my hero, face-to-face, separated only by the proffered autograph book. He had just made his Test debut, against New Zealand, and was to play one further Test that summer, suffering the dismay of being torn apart by a 21-year-old left-handed whippersnapper named Graeme Pollock. He consequently missed the 1965-66 tour of Australia, something which years later he still described as the greatest disappointment of his career.

The following summer perhaps encapsulated the roller-coaster character of Snow's career better than most. Already, his frustrations with the Sussex Committee were making themselves evident, and after one altercation with the county captain, 'Tiger' Pataudi, John was summoned before that body – not for the last time. But his answers came in performance. On a Saturday morning at Hove, 10,000 people packed in to see the county play the West Indian tourists, a magnetic attraction. But they left the ground not knowing whether to be delighted or disappointed that they had seen the visitors bowled out on a green top for just 123, the lithe and inspired J.A. Snow taking 7 for 29, figures which remained the best of his career until he surpassed them with eight wickets against Middlesex at headquarters nine years later. That devastating display brought Snow back into the England team for the last three Tests of the summer – and there he stayed, merit-wise, until 1973. The only occasions when he missed Test matches were for reasons of fitness or, on a number of occasions, discipline.

Strange, really, that a passage in the Oval Test of that 1966 series may be more entrenched in the minds of cricket followers than any other Snow contribution. Strange, because he was batting at the time. It was that remarkable last wicket stand of 128 with the plodding, lugubrious Ken Higgs which took Snow's posed picture on to the front pages, not any triumph with the new ball. He was proud of it, nonetheless, and so was I, sitting riveted to the television screen in the last week of what seemed an endlessly sunny summer holiday. It had been a memorable holiday. The first two Tests, watched live, of my young life. I was at Lord's, distraught that Snow was absent, and at The Oval for a day. A tragedy, I thought at the time, that it had to be the wrong day.

There can surely be no doubt that Snow was by then England's most potent weapon. Yet in Pakistan, during the hastily arranged tour in 1969 which replaced the scheduled visit to South Africa, he was dropped because of his apparently insubordinate attitude. He wrote a poem about the ritual, called simply *On Being Dropped*:

Standing
on a still summers day,
eye watching swallows
earth-hugging
insect-chasing way,
wondering what to do,
knowing that it always happens
and now it's happened to you. . .

John had two collections of poems published, *Contrasts* (Fuller d'Arch Smith) in 1971, and *Moments and Thoughts* (Kaye and Ward) in 1973. Many related to cricket, others to life and love, but the best-known, if not the best, recalls his thoughts in the build-up to playing for England at headquarters. He called it *Lord's Test* and it begins:

Tomorrow starts the night before
lying looking through the blackness
wondering about the hidden day
'til falling forward trackless
unknowing down the slope,
you're there sitting in it,
you and hope.

There were more triumphs to come at Lord's when that was
written; none, maybe, to match the period which will surely be
remembered as the pinnacle of his career, when his bowling did so
much to bring home the Ashes from the 1970-71 tour. He took 31
wickets, found himself the central figure of a potential riot after he
hit Terry Jenner on the head, was involved in a series of rows with
umpire Lou Rowan, and ended up in hospital after crashing
fingers-first into a fence. But he came home a hero, and rightly so.

Sussex dropped him the following summer, for 'not trying', and
his relationship with the county was never again sweet, despite the
resuscitation applied by Tony Greig when he took over as captain.
It was Greig, too, who recalled Snow to the England side for his
swansong, during 1975 and 1976, but not before yet more inci-
dents to justify the title of his autobiography, *Cricket Rebel*.

He has never tried to wriggle out of blame for the barging over
of little Sunil Gavaskar in 1971. He knew at the instant of contact
that he would be dropped for it and, in retrospect, he pondered
only on the fanciful thought that things might have been different
if Gavaskar had been a stone or two heavier. It was, however,
another nail in Snow's coffin so far as certain administrators were
concerned. Some wanted to do much more than leave him out of
the next Test. There were those who would never again have
countenanced his presence in an England side. An hysterical
reaction, maybe, but to a degree they had their way. Snow was
ditched by England while he was still the best around, and it took
Greig, whose selections were always influenced much more by
ability than personality, to bring him back.

There was, he will admit, something about Lord's which always
inspired him, and he proved it twice more. In 1975, he brought
the Australians to their knees by lunch on the second day and
Greig, for one, recalls the reception for the England team in the

packed pavilion as 'the most emotional moment of my cricketing life'. Then, a year later and against an all-conquering West Indies side, Snow and Derek Underwood conspired to gain England what seemed a decisive lead before a massed Friday crowd. My enduring memory of the man will be of that evening. Alcohol and euphoria were having their way, the Tavern area was crazily crammed and a noisy rendition of 'Rule Britannia' was underway. Snow, in the vest he always wore to bowl, clutching a beer, appeared on the dressing-room balcony. The singing was interrupted for several minutes of cheering. They even sang 'For He's a Jolly Good Fellow'. There were still those at Lord's who thought he was nothing of the sort but maybe, just for a night, they felt forgiving enough to join in. It was, after all, virtually the end of the road for a very great fast bowler.

A travel agent now, and part-time journalist, Snow is husband and father, an altogether less explosive character than many will remember but still critical of certain administrative systems within the game he still, in his own way, loves. John Snow's name will conjure up many different visions to many different people. He will not kid himself into thinking they will all be affectionate, either. But surely, above all, he was a truly great fast bowler. We have not seen too many of his like in England recently.

Dennis Lillee

PAUL WEAVER

I didn't like him at first. For this schoolboy of the Sussex '60s there was only one fast bowler – John Snow – and the emergence of Dennis Lillee was a threat to that private, prejudiced, insular world of hero-worship. By 1970 Snow had established himself as the finest fast bowler in the world. Moody and magnificent, a rebel with or without a cause, Snow inspired awe with the smooth menace of his bowling and his (occasionally) athletic fielding in the Hove deep, where he would stand with hands on hips and a poet's nose thrown high as if to scent a passing sonnet. The end of that year marked the peak of Snow's career, with his 31 wickets in the Ashes series in Australia. But that was the same winter that a raw, tearaway fast bowler called Lillee began to cause such a stir in Western Australia that he played in two Tests in that series and at once impressed Snow with his natural speed and action.

At 21, Lillee was eight years younger than Snow and not yet in the same class as a bowler. But it was a different story when the pair next met in England in 1972. Early that year I met Peter Parfitt in a London hospital, where he had just had a cartilage operation. His left-handed batting was to be used in three Tests against Australia that year, and he had followed the progress of Lillee closely. 'Obviously he is some prospect', said Parfitt. 'But I will be very, very surprised if he is anywhere near as good as Snowy.' To our mutual consternation, Lillee proved every bit as good as the England spearhead that summer, as both bowlers enjoyed a marvellous series that was drawn 2-2. And if Lillee pulled level with Snow that year, his subsequent deeds have established him as the greatest fast bowler of the modern era – possibly of any era.

Lillee retired from Test cricket in January 1984, and typically he left the stage with yet another match-winning performance. He captured Pakistan's last four wickets for just 22 runs in 58 balls to

Dennis Lillee

give Australia a surprisingly comfortable ten-wicket win in the fifth Test in Sydney. When he led Australia from the field at the end of his 70th and final Test a spectator from the famous Sydney Hill draped over his right shoulder a huge green flag with the familiar golden boxing kangaroo. It was then that the crowd erupted, for the last time, with the old war cry of 'Lil-lee . . . Lil-lee . . .' At 34, he had finished his stupendous career with a world record 355 wickets for an average of 23.92. Never again will we see that drooping black moustache, that warrior's headband and that dynamic, shoulder-swinging run-up which preceded a classic fast bowler's action.

The 'macho' aggression he brought to his cricket often spilled over into unforgivable excesses, like the kick he aimed at Pakistan's Javed Miandad. Sometimes it was just plain foolishness – like the time he held up play with an aluminium bat. Even in that farewell appearance against Pakistan he showed unreasonable dissent when umpire Mel Johnson gave Abdul Qadir not out after an appeal for a catch behind (television replays proved that the umpire had got a difficult decision right). Lillee's outrages could never be condoned, although the notoriously weak-kneed Australian cricket authorities always encouraged bad behaviour by their flaccid indifference just when hard-line action was called for. But while Lillee's actions betrayed a possible character flaw, this could never detract from his pure bowling greatness. He was the best, and despite all his oaths and airs that was always his main weapon of intimidation. That aggressive streak, his piratical, insatiable appetite for more victims and his proud refusal to be dominated was always worth a wicket or two even before he took the ball in his hand. It was certainly enough to frighten the flannels off any newcomer, and I well remember the young Tony Greig – himself to become an exceptional competitor – nervously chain-smoking his way through a packet of 20 as he waited to go out and bat against the demon at Lord's in 1972.

Lillee's record is all the more remarkable because he never had an equally durable opening partner to keep the pressure on at the other end. Jeff Thomson, for a while, looked as though he would link up with Lillee to form a partnership as potent as the Ray Lindwall-Keith Miller combination a generation before. Lillee and Thomson were virtually unplayable on the fast Australian wickets in the winter of 1974-75, when England were over-whelmed 4-1. But Thomson was a sensational rather than a great bowler, spectacularly fast on occasions but lacking the consistent control – and fitness – which he needed to sustain him as Lillee's foil. Not that Lillee was exactly injury-free. In fact his immense triumph of will over injury is almost as remarkable as his record. He was out of action for almost two years with a fractured ver-tebra, and everyone but himself considered his career at a close in the mid-70s. But he saw specialist after specialist, gritted his teeth through the pain and refused to take no for an answer.

He returned even better than before. The half-yard he had lost in raw pace was more than compensated for by a higher degree of control in his swing and cut and a more refined ability within himself to bowl. He developed such variety of menace that his threat was still as great as ever when I watched him make his last Test tour of England in 1981. The bald patch and the arm, not quite as high as before, failed to disguise his enduring devilry. I watched him bowl Australia to the brink of victory on a dead Oval wicket which helped to evoke rich nostalgia, with a century from Geoff Boycott and a match-saving innings from Alan Knott. I watched him with Bob Willis, England's leading fast bowler, who three years later was to become his country's leading wicket-taker. 'That man is remarkable', said Willis, in his familiar monotone, shaking his head in slow disbelief. 'He can bowl anything. He's certainly the greatest fast bowler I've seen – probably the best of all time. I certainly can't imagine anyone having been better than him.'

Lillee the showman was made to measure when Kerry Packer burst upon cricket with an explosion of razzmatazz and marketing expertise in 1977. He was king of the ring in Packer's travelling cricket circus, but floodlit games, white balls and pyjamas of various colours never undermined his combative nature as he found himself up against some of the world's greatest cricketers – Barry Richards, Viv Richards, Clive Lloyd, Imran Khan and many more. He was still Australia's number one player when cricket returned to normal in 1979. All he lost was two years' Test cricket which could have taken his final wicket aggregate to an unassailable-looking 400 plus.

As it was, he retired with Willis, Ian Botham and Kapil Dev

hard on the heels of his record. And remember that Willis and Botham both picked up 'easy' wickets against Packer-depleted countries between 1977-79. But whatever these three bowlers finish with, not one would ever claim to be in Lillee's class as a bowler. With Greg Chappell and Rodney Marsh, Lillee was a cornerstone of the Australian sides of the 1970s and early 1980s. And it was no coincidence that Chappell and Marsh followed their friend into retirement almost immediately. With Lillee gone, an era had ended and the team had to be rebuilt. At least Lillee left Australia with the world's leading white fast bowler, Geoff Lawson, if you regard the rather Lillee-like Richard Hadlee as an all-rounder.

It was so different when Lillee broke into the side in 1970. 'Garth' McKenzie had gone some time before, and for years the Australian public had cried out for a new fast bowler capable of returning the fire-power of the West Indies, England and South Africa. Lillee arrived almost as if the hungry minds of the Australians had willed him into being. And when he arrived he found his ideal captain in Ian Chappell, a man after his own aggressive heart who was to bully and bend him towards greatness. It was the elder Chappell brother who honed and directed Lillee's already mean cricketing mind.

Lillee was an old-fashioned fast bowler; a physical batsman-hater whose overt aggression always concealed a subtler science. He was also a very modern cricketer, not only with his off-field dress but with his hostile attitude towards authorities lesser players would never have questioned. He often seemed genuinely surprised by his own follies, for instance in 1981 in Leeds, when he backed England at 500-1 to beat Australia in that incredible Botham-Willis Test. There was never any suggestion of under-handedness, just astonishment at his remarkable lack of sensitivity. But I don't want to remember Lillee as a particularly sensitive creature. I like to remember him – even bowling against the Poms – as the greatest fast bowler of my time. I want to recall that 'macho' approach, with the trunk thrown forward, the shoulders swinging venomously and the dark hair trailing behind. Whenever he bowled against England I was faced with the old, classic dilemma. I wanted to see his rich talent draw its full reward while, somehow, England thrived against the bowlers at the other end.

I met him for the first time in 1981 when I asked him for an interview for my newspaper, and was pleasantly surprised when he gave me considerable time without ever asking for money. And my delight was complete when he talked with reverence about another of my heroes, Snow. 'He was the most skilful England fast bowler I ever saw', he said. 'And I will always be grateful to him because he taught me how to bowl my leg-cutter.' You see, even heroes have their heroes. . .

Bob Taylor

MICHAEL CAREY

'Robert Taylor is a true gentleman, a fine artist and tactful and kind.' Those words were written long ago, not about Bob Taylor, but about the other Robert Taylor, the Hollywood film star, of course; yet they seem curiously appropriate to the man who has kept wicket for Derbyshire since 1961 and, as I write, is about to add to his total of 54 Test match appearances for England.

It is not easy to retain a sense of values in today's frenzied, nerve-racked and often over-commercialised world of sport, but I believe that Bob Taylor has managed to do so more than most. He remains as affable and approachable now, even at the end of the most demanding or frustrating day, as he was when he was making his way in the game. It is impossible to find anyone with a harsh word to say about him; not that one wants to. As a wicket-keeper he has, of course, honed and polished his technique to a degree of perfection that makes a likely successor for the England side difficult to spot, even though he is in his 43rd year. I think I am correct in saying that had he not been selected to play for England in the 1983 Test series against New Zealand, he would have accepted that his international career was over and would have taken that as the cue to make a graceful exit from the county scene, too.

However, the selectors wisely realised there was no immediate, ready-made replacement and Taylor carried on, as ever paying special attention to his fitness and physique, well aware that this does much to keep the reflexes sharp. On an England tour it is not unusual to find him still training long after the others have departed for a shower and a drink, putting in that little bit extra that the over-40s need to keep in trim.

Off the field, too, he appreciates the need to conserve his energies. An evening abroad with no official function to attend will usually find him doing nothing more extravagant than having

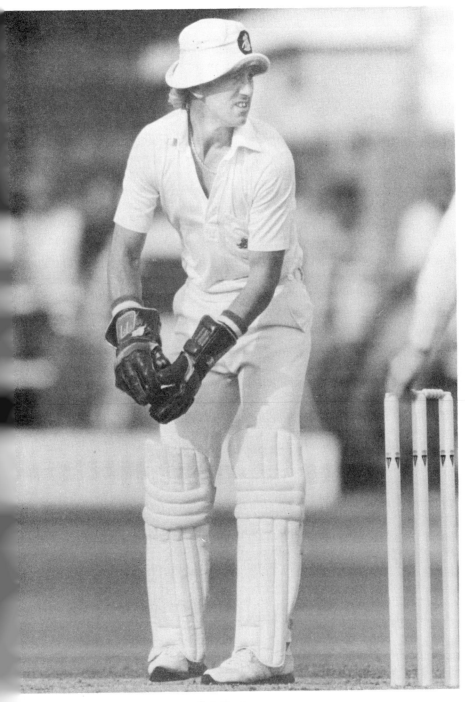

Bob Taylor

a quiet meal and then adjourning to his room to keep up to date with his correspondence. Question him about it and he will look you in the eye and say: 'Well, there's another day's cricket to get through tomorrow, isn't there?'. Another day's cricket. I think that tends to over-simplify the attitude to keeping wicket that Taylor has adopted, ever since the day, when making his debut for Bignall End in the North Staffordshire and South Cheshire League, he walked in to bat wearing black plimsolls, grey trousers and pads up to his thighs and had to admit to an umpire enquiring whether he was wearing a 'box' that he did not know what it was!

To Taylor, I sense that every day spent in the middle is one to be relished and appreciated in the knowledge that it will soon be gone forever, and that nothing less than 100 per cent endeavour and application will do. The fact that he still managed to maintain these standards during an era when his country were producing some of the most dismal cricket seen anywhere (in matching surroundings) has always seemed to me a graphic illustration of the character of a man determined never to let his level of efficiency suffer because of the deficiencies of others.

All too often in those days, Bob's performance behind the stumps would produce an isolated note of cheer for Derbyshire's long-suffering supporters. Sometimes, I fear, we were all a little guilty of taking him for granted. He was so unobtrusively efficient you forgot he was there, like a good football referee. There were times, too, when his lack of exhibitionism, his distaste for anything flash, tended to camouflage a particularly brilliant piece of work. At close of play in the bar, in fact, it became almost a ritual to say to someone, by way of passing the time of day: 'Bob kept well again today'. They would nod in agreement and you would then press on to other, more indeterminate matters, knowing full well that Bob would keep well the next day and the one after that. He was the one consistent thread running through a dreadful period for Derbyshire, yet he never complained unreasonably, rocked the boat (it was leaky enough anyway!) or sought to take his talents elsewhere.

He was so undemonstrative (perhaps to his own cost, when selectors and others were watching) that I suspect that only Taylor himself, and possibly a bowler or two, recognised when he was having a rare bad day. After some years of watching Derbyshire

up and down the country, it was possible to detect a missed chance
or error by watching to see if his head went down immediately
afterwards. Later I discovered that while this was by no means a
bad way of interpreting events from some of our less than strategi-
cally placed Press boxes, it was Taylor's way of willing himself to
concentrate on the next ball, rather than hanging his head in
shame. At Ilkeston, that ground of mixed memory, he once
dropped Roy Fredericks three times in one over while standing up
to Ian Buxton, who was bowling a fairly lavish away-swing to the
left-hander. Buxton can still be persuaded to chunter about this
when he calls in to watch Derbyshire these days. At the time,
though, I doubt if more than a handful of people on the ground
realised it. Not everyone would have classed the 'misses' as anything more than technical chances. Taylor, however, would not
spare himself. He admitted later: 'I knew my concentration was
not right, possibly because it was a Sunday match in the middle of
an MCC game in which I was playing and I had allowed myself to
become too casual'.

   Taylor will discuss wicket-keeping only in terms of standing up
– 'Any decent slip fielder could do it standing back', he has a habit
of saying. Indeed, the times he has dropped catches off the
quicker bowlers seem to occur about as often as eclipses of the sun
and become just as much of a talking point. Once, during the
pre-lunch session of a Benson and Hedges match at Derby, he
appeared to drop a fairly straightforward outside edge off Alan
Ward. In the Press box, the occupants exchanged glances. Had
they really seen what they thought they had seen? In those days
the players had to pass close by on their way to lunch and the safest
thing, before announcing this sensation to the outside world, it
was agreed, was to check it with one of the protagonists. Ward
himself was asked and his historic reply is quoted to this day in the
Press boxes of Derbyshire: 'You know, I couldn't believe it myself
so I had to go and ask Bob at the end of the over if the bloke really
had hit it. He had'.

   While there are those who used to – and still do – offer me
sympathy at spending my formative cricket-writing years watching Derbyshire, rather as people are criticised for playing snooker
in their youth, I have no regrets. An awful lot of know-how and
advice was dispensed in the pavilion bars of England in those days

by people like Taylor. Some of it seems to have stuck and it is pleasant to think that writers like myself may once have helped to salvage his career.

Exactly 20 years ago, he missed the start of the season with a football injury (he was with Port Vale for a time). To avoid complications, Taylor told the club he had slipped in the escalator in Lewis's department store in Hanley – a likely story! – and Laurie Johnston played as a batsman-wicket-keeper. He did well enough to tempt Derbyshire to hint that they might leave Taylor out indefinitely. Ruefully telling the story against himself now, Taylor recalls that he seriously, if a shade impetuously, contemp- lated giving up county cricket there and then if they did. To a side with Derbyshire's familiar batting problems, a young, specialist wicket-keeper was probably something of a luxury. The club, however, were reminded by myself and others of where we thought their priorities should lie. Taylor was eventually rein- stated and in 1984 remains, remarkably, only Derbyshire's third full-time wicket-keeper since the war, after Harry Elliott and George Dawkes.

Obviously, the end is now not far away for him, but you can be sure that when he goes it will be with dignity. At county level, it will be his decision. He will know when his standards have started to decline below what he considers to be an acceptable level – as they did, temporarily, when he was made captain of Derbyshire in the mid-70s. Though it was hard to detect from the boundary edge, Taylor said the job had affected his wicket-keeping. I dare say it will be similarly hard to notice any decline when his retire- ment comes. 'I am a professional, others rely on me and it is a crime to let them down', he is fond of saying.

As Ronald Reagan, no less, once said of that other Robert Taylor: 'Perhaps each of us has his own memory, but somehow they all add up to "nice man" '. In Bob Taylor's case, no one would argue with that.

Stuart Turner

DAVID LEMMON

There was always much laughter from his net at the Ilford Cricket School, yet the faint-hearted believed that you had to be a masochist to want to be a member of his group. Those he coached were invariably the more serious club cricketers, and they loved his caustic wit, professional approach, complete commitment and total dedication. 'What was that, Keith?' would suddenly boom out. 'What are you playing at? I don't expect that to bowl you!' He whipped his arm over from where he was standing by the bowling stump and his delivery sent the batsman's off-stump rocking on its spring base. 'I expect this to bowl you.' And the stump rocked again. He wasn't putting on a show. He was seriously applying himself to the art of coaching cricket and his charges responded to his passion and determination with a sense of awe, gratitude and unbounded respect. For Stuart Turner had come to coaching, as to cricket, the hard way. Everything he has achieved in the game has been hard earned. He became an advanced coach when there were very few qualified at that level. He became a cricketer in spite of initial rejection.

His father was a publisher's representative with a passionate love of cricket. He planted the seeds of interest in his son and it was from his father that Stuart Turner learned all he knew about the game. The only thing that he ever wanted to be was a professional cricketer and for the realisation of that ambition he had to suffer much. His performances in club cricket with Buckhurst Hill brought him to the notice of Essex and they engaged him. He made his first-class debut at Bradford towards the end of July, 1965, and was nearly knocked out by Freddie Trueman. He played in eight more matches that season, but was not seen again until 1968. In fact, he had not been re-engaged. When he arrived at the County Ground for pre-season training in 1966, he was greeted by an embarrassed Trevor Bailey who told him that the

Stuart Turner

Club thought he had been informed that his contract was not being renewed.

Newly-married, a dream shattered, jobless and somewhat embittered, he needed and sought quick employment. In Essex, in the 60s, if not now, there was always work to be had at Ford's, and that is where he went. Ford's, like many large firms, held inter-departmental cricket tournaments, played on a weekly basis in the evenings between sides composed in equal quantities of those who knew the game and those, kitless, who had been coerced into making up the numbers. Half-measures were not for Stuart. Within a week he had shaped his department's team into a fighting cricket unit, the like of which Ford's had never seen before. They swept all before them. 'He made us into a cricket team', says a friend from that time. 'It had always been a joke. Now it was fun, but it was also serious and I don't think any of us had ever enjoyed a sport so much before, nor have we enjoyed one so much since.'

Turner thrived in club cricket, and in 1968 he was invited to rejoin Essex, now sharpened and streamlined under Brian Taylor, a man who, in terms of cricket, spoke the same language. He hit a maiden century at Ilford, against Glamorgan, that year and took 29 wickets. Two years later, when he hit a career best 121 at Taunton, he was awarded his county cap. He was already 27 years old, but now surely he would establish himself in the first-class game.

At The Oval in 1971 he bowled Storey and had both Long and Jackman caught behind to complete the hat-trick. The Essex County handbook failed to record this feat, one of only 15 instances in the history of the Club. *Wisden* wrote of him that he 'again failed to produce the form of which he looked capable'.

The following season, in a Benson and Hedges match at Lord's, he bowled a menacing spell of 11 overs in which he conceded only 28 runs. Four straightforward catches were put down off his bowling, so that he alone of the main bowlers remained wicketless. After lunch he sprinted 30 yards round the square-leg boundary to catch Mike Brearley, splendidly, in front of the Mound Stand. The score-board credited the catch to John Lever and *Wisden* has perpetuated that error. Essex faced 232 and he came in at 71 for 5. He was bowled second ball by Fred Titmus. It was, I think, the lowest point of his career. He was close to tears when he said afterwards 'I don't know where the next wicket or the next run is coming from'.

When there were moments of glory that year they were short-lived. At Leyton, he faced Graham McKenzie of Leicestershire with the second new ball and he hit a cover drive which I have never seen equalled. It was a breathtaking shot, all power and majesty, and it rocketed into the fence. He was caught at slip next ball. 'I was still thinking about that shot', he said, somewhat ruefully, in the bar later. It seemed that the fates were conspiring against him at Leyton that week for in the second match, against Worcestershire, he achieved an early breakthrough when he had Headley taken at slip. He then bowled magnificently on a perfect wicket as Turner and Parker, the two New Zealanders, joined in an unmemorable stand of 220. Chances were missed off him and he had nothing to show for his labours. As the 85th over approached and the scramble for bonus points began, he was replaced by Boyce and Lever. Worcestershire engaged in mass suicide. Grotesque shots brought wickets in the mad rush. Boyce and Lever finished with eight wickets between them. Turner watched his friends and could have mused on Brian Taylor's assertion relating to the nonsense of averages: 'It isn't how you bowl sometimes; it's *when* you bowl that matters'.

The struggle for success, to be accepted as a *first-class* cricketer, and the buffets he received hardened Stuart in those earlier years. He has never suffered fools or sycophants gladly. He became abrasive, and he clashed with authority, but those who knew him well, and his loyalty to his team and his colleagues, adored him. Above all, the Essex crowd loved him.

Perhaps his constant endeavour – he bristles with it as he runs up to bowl – fingered a strain in people, and if there had been an election among the supporters to name Taylor's successor as Essex captain, it is likely that Stuart Turner would have won it; the supporters' magazine at the time suggested as much. Not that he ever coveted such an honour, he didn't, and it is doubtful whether such a choice would have been a wise one. The agony of wholehearted commitment and total emotional involvement are not the best qualities for captaincy however much they endear themselves to the human heart. But Stuart Turner touches chords of forgotten aspirations. He scurries up to bowl with that purposeful stride only, to lose the fluency momentarily at the last as he lurches out of his hips in delivery. His bat is big. His stance is staunch, emanating power, but the eagerness to hit offers a vulnerability.

His qualities have sought the heroic for which his technique has not always been sufficient, but such have been the endeavours that he has touched the heights, albeit on a smaller stage than most players. At Colchester, in 1975, he hit Underwood for two sixes in the final over, the 100th of the innings, to bring up the 300 and the fourth batting point, but those who were not at Castle Park that day will never realise, nor ever read about, the grandeur of that 23 not out by the Essex number seven.

There were disappointments in plenty, too, most of them not personal, but bound up in the team's craving for success and the passing years. And then, more relaxed, with an easier rhythm and fluency of delivery in his bowling and disciplined aggression in his batting, he became the outstanding all-rounder in England in 1974. He scored 963 runs, took 73 wickets and made 11 catches. He won the Wetherall Award as the best all-rounder and came very, very close to being selected to go to Australia with Mike Denness's team. 'If he could have turned some of those eighties into hundreds,' said one selector, 'he would have gone.' But then he was usually batting at number seven or eight and the side required him to make brisk eighties rather than prolonged hundreds; and he has never seen cricket as anything but a team game.

He has never got so close to the England side since. One Test umpire remarked that had he not upset one or two people when he was younger, he would certainly have played for his country in limited-over internationals, for Stuart Turner has thrived on the one-day game. His relentless accuracy as a bowler, his aggression as a batsman and his exuberance in the field are qualities ideally suited to instant cricket and he became the first bowler to reach 200 wickets in the John Player League.

Yet still the ultimate success eluded him and Essex. Some years ago, Mike Brearley commented on how good a bowler Stuart Turner was and how strong a side Essex would be with more substance at number five. It was a wise prophecy, but there were still more agonies to come before it was completely fulfilled.

After missing out on the England tour to Australia in 1974-75, Turner went to South Africa with D.H. Robins' team and he returned there in 1976-77 and again the following year, helping Natal to the Currie Cup in his first year and to the Datsun Shield in his second. But still nothing with Essex. In 1978, they chased Kent all the way in the race for the County Championship, but they finished as runners-up, the highest position in their history. Even more agonising was their defeat in the semi-final of the Gillette Cup. When Somerset batted, Stuart Turner bowled six successive maidens to Brian Rose, but when Richards savaged him in two overs Fletcher rather unwisely took Turner out of the attack and did not bring him back to finish his quota of overs when Richards had gone. As Essex desperately chased runs Turner hit Botham for two incredibly bizarre and unorthodox fours before being bowled for 12 when attempting another. Neil Smith was run out on the last ball of the match going for the third run which would have given Essex victory. Stuart was meant to drive the Club van back to Chelmsford that night, but when he got into the driver's seat he was so dejected, so emotionally drained, that he shook his head and Brian Hardie took over. It seemed to all then that the last chance for glory had gone.

The defeat at Taunton was all the more shattering because the year before they had gone to Scarborough in the penultimate match of the John Player League needing only to win to take the title. They had been beaten only once in the season, and when they scored 178 for 7 and reduced Yorkshire to 92 for 4 off 26 overs, the title appeared to be within their grasp. Turner had bowled with his usual nagging accuracy and economy until, in his last over, Bairstow had attacked him and won the game for Yorkshire. Essex were devastated and Turner sank in the corner of the dressing-room, taking all the blame upon himself, before Fletcher and his team-mates consoled him. Then came 1979.

Stuart Turner had been a capped player for nine years; so had John Lever, but as Turner was the older, now 36, it was agreed that he should have the benefit in 1979. It all began well. He hit the first six of the season, at Fenner's in April, and then he hit 102, the fourth century of his career, in under two hours against Kent in the opening Championship game. It heralded Essex's *annus mirabilis* – and Turner's.

In the Benson and Hedges Cup semi-final at Chelmsford, Lumb and Hampshire had begun Yorkshire's innings with a stand of 107 which was ended when Turner took a superb running catch at long-on to end Hampshire's knock. Yorkshire had then stumbled to 173 for 9 from their 55 overs. Essex lost Lilley in the second over and then hesitated nervously towards victory. They were 139 for 6 when Stuart came in, but he and Keith Pont added 30 before Pont's fine innings came to an end, and Smith hit the winning four. He and Stuart ran from the field with their arms round each other.

Stuart Turner had always said, not with a great deal of conviction, 'If we could only reach a final, it wouldn't matter if we won or not, but just to play in front of a packed house at Lord's would be wonderful'. The wonder arrived – Essex's day of triumph after 103 years of waiting – and he was part of it. Two months later they added the County Championship and his benefit broke Essex records. He had been a good and faithful servant, and the crowd knew it.

Essex cricket now moved into a new era and what must surely be the last phase of Stuart Turner's career began. There were more honours; another County Championship, the elusive John Player League at last, and two appearances in the Benson and Hedges final. For Stuart, there were individual awards. Three Benson and Hedges Gold Awards came his way, one of them after a spell of bowling at Canterbury in the semi-final in 1983 which frustrated Kent to destruction. Perhaps more typical was the one he won at Chelmsford in 1982, when Essex beat Hampshire by one wicket in a match which had no bearing on who would qualify for the quarter-finals. Essex had had a disastrous start to the season and their depression continued when, having bowled Hampshire out for 130, they found themselves at 14 for 6. Then Turner came in and scored 55 not out to win the match.

He is always at his best in such circumstances; his runs have been scored and his wickets taken when they were most needed. The abrasive man of earlier years has now mellowed. He is a support to younger players, rich in humour as his side is rich in humour, and he has the respect of all. When Access gave Essex a celebration dinner for winning the County Championship in 1983 he was cheered as he was presented; and when Brian Hardie had his benefit dinner at Lord's, it was Stuart who conducted the auction after the meal, raising much money for his friend.

His popularity with supporters has increased with the years, for if one man can be said to have encapsulated the strivings of Essex and the longings of their followers, it is Stuart Turner. There were occasions in 1982 and 1983 when, with the advent of young players such as Neil Foster and Derek Pringle, he was left out of the side, but he accepted the role of 12th man with typical zest and at the end of the 1983 season it was he who achieved the breakthrough in the vital last game with Yorkshire.

Two years before, at Hove, when Essex were playing Sussex in the quarter-final of the NatWest Trophy, he chased a ball, unsuccessfully, to the fine-leg boundary. As he raced to the fence, the ball ahead of him, a voice from the business tent on the boundary was heard to shout 'You're too old, Turner'. 'I knew I'd hear it one day,' he said afterwards, 'but I thought that's it.' He bowled the next over from the opposite end and dismissed Gould and Imran and swung the game in Essex's favour. In 1984, aged 41, Stuart Turner is starting another season, and there are many who think that he will never be too old.

I suppose he isn't really the stuff of a hero. He's never played in a Test match, and he never will, and his records of runs and wickets have been bettered by many. But then Arthur Miller's Willy Loman in *Death of a Salesman* was denied heroic status by some critics because he wasn't a prince or a lord. So may it be with Stuart Turner. Yet, if the county game is the essence of cricket, all that is good and true away from the fanfare of the Test arena, then Stuart Turner is at the very heart of the sport. It is the three-day game upon which all our first-class cricket has been founded, and its honest practitioners should be those we admire most. There may have been better cricketers than Stuart Turner, but there have been none more honest in endeavour, and that endeavour has brought pleasure to many, not least of all myself.

Sunil Gavaskar

DICKY RUTNAGUR

The triumph of youth is always stirring and therefore it was small wonder that the cricketing world was agog when, in 1971, Sunil Manohar Gavaskar, just 21 and recently graduated from Bombay University, amassed 774 runs in four Test matches, and that against such formidable opponents as the West Indies. When Gavaskar was picked for that tour, he had played just four first-class matches, and if his name was known at all abroad, it was only to members of the London Schools team that toured India in 1965.

The Indian team which visited the West Indies in 1971 contained nine first-time tourists, but Gavaskar was one of only two specialist batsmen in the party who had not yet played in a Test match. The bright young hope of that side was Gundappa Viswanath, who was Gavaskar's contemporary in age, but who was already an acknowledged star after scoring a century in his debut against Australia in the previous series. It was ironic that the touring party included six batsmen – Gavaskar being one – each of whom, at some stage, opened a Test innings, and yet the most glaring of its shortcomings was its weakness at the top of the batting order.

The Indians had to live with this problem until the first Test, which Gavaskar missed because he was unfit. By his own admission, he had been biting his nails during the last exciting days before the team's departure and had developed a whitlow which became so inflamed during the long journey that he had to undergo surgery while the team made an overnight stop in New York. The attending surgeon said that had another 24 hours elapsed the only cure for Gavaskar's ailment would have been amputation of the middle finger of his left hand. Gavaskar's nerves may have been wound up while he packed his bags, but once in the West Indies he was perfectly relaxed. He was exhilarated by the throbbing rhythms of calypso and reggae and

Sunil Gavaskar

altogether revelled in the fresh experiences of a first tour. His batting did not have the poise that came later with maturity, yet it did not betray the slightest trace of tension.

India made the West Indies follow on in the first Test, for which Gavaskar could not be considered. Nevertheless, their prospects for the forthcoming matches did not look good. Ashok Mankad, their first choice opening batsman, had looked vulnerable against top pace in the early matches, although it was not for this reason that he was left out of the first Test. Abid Ali and Jayantilal, who eventually opened in the first Test, were easily overwhelmed. Wadekar, the captain, who batted at number three, was in no sort of form and worse still, Viswanath had sustained a knee injury which would keep him out until at least the third Test. If the Indians left Jamaica without their reputation suffering serious damage, it was only because Dilip Sardesai, who was selected mainly because of his experience and was, in fact, one of the last two players to be picked, immediately hit masterly form.

This was the grim background against which Gavaskar played his maiden first-class innings of the tour, against the Leeward Islands, on a two-paced pitch at St Kitts. Although his injury had given him little scope for practice in the nets, in scoring 82 and 32 not out, he played with an authority and ease which were beyond any of his team-mates. A long sequence of big scores followed: 125 and 63 against Trinidad; 65 and 67 in the second Test, which produced India's first-ever win over the West Indies; 116 and 64 in the third Test; 67 against Barbados and 117 in the fourth Test. Gavaskar made only 14 and 12 against the Windward Islands, but in the six-day fifth Test, he achieved the rare distinction of scoring a century and a double-century in the same match. This feat had been performed only once before, by Doug Walters, and has been repeated just twice since, by Lawrence Rowe and Greg Chappell. India finished on top in that drawn final Test, but they had been 166 runs behind on the first innings and, without either of Gavaskar's contributions, they would surely have lost.

Gavaskar batted for six hours and 40 minutes for his 124 in the first innings and eight hours and 50 minutes for his 220 in the second. It was astonishing that a young man of such small stature and so limited in experience could apply himself hour after hour. His marathon was even more remarkable for the fact that the two nights that fell during the time-span of his innings provided little rest as Gavaskar was kept awake by a violent toothache. He resisted taking any pain-killing treatment lest it made him drowsy or slowed down his reflexes. At the end of the series, Gavaskar had a Bradmanesque average of 154.80. It was inevitable that a Test career launched with such momentum should culminate, almost 13 years later, in a list of centuries longer than that of any batsman before him.

In his 99th Test Gavaskar scored his 30th century to break Sir Donald Bradman's record. He had scaled another peak earlier in the same series, against the West Indies, when he accumulated the highest number of Test runs ever recorded, surpassing Geoff Boycott. Of all opening batsmen in Test history, only six have career averages higher than Gavaskar's 52.46, but of those who batted more than 20 innings, he has only three superiors, Sutcliffe, Hobbs and Hutton.

It has often been said, unfairly, of Gavaskar that the reluctance of Indian umpires to give him out has been an aid to the accumulation of such a mass of runs. But the fact is that, having played one fewer Test abroad than at home, he has made 50 more runs and two more centuries on foreign soil than on his own. His runs have been earned against some of the greatest exponents of pace and swing in the game's history; the likes of Sobers, Snow, Willis, Hadlee, Roberts, Holding, Lillee, Thomson, Botham, Imran Khan and Marshall. Moreover, as their opponents have never had to fear retaliation, India's batsmen have always been at the receiving end of some of the most intimidatory bowling that any country has had to endure since Bodyline.

With a big innings by Gavaskar or the early capture of his wicket so crucial to the fate of a Test match, he has always been the target of the heaviest flak. Still, he never felt the need for any form of protective headgear until he was nearly 34. Even now, he does not wear a helmet or visor, but a small guard for his temples, which he tucks into his wide-brimmed cloth hat. He may not have resorted even to this small precaution had he not decided to re-introduce the hook into his repertoire of strokes. Gavaskar has not escaped being hit on the head or in the face. But if he has been undermined at all, it has been as a result of what is known in the trade as the 'knuckle ball'. Despite the fact that the most prolific run-getter of all time, Don Bradman, was a man of short stature, there has always been a conflict of opinion as to whether lack of inches is an advantage or a disadvantage in playing quick bowling.

In Gavaskar's case, it would seem to have been a disadvantage, judging by the frequency with which he has been caught off the glove or the shoulder of the bat – as often as not from balls which lesser batsmen would have got nowhere near touching. In this respect, Gavaskar has had more problems in Australia than any- where else, due to the extra bounce its pitches afford. He has made three tours of Australia, achieving varying degrees of success. The first was with the Rest of the World team that filled in for the barred South Africans in 1971-72. Gavaskar was, at that stage, too young and inexperienced to do himself justice against a rampant Dennis Lillee, then at his fastest. Six years later, in his first Test series in Australia, Gavaskar made three centuries in consecutive Tests. It is significant, however, that they were all scored in the second innings when the pitches had lost their initial freshness and resilience. His second series in Australia, a short one of three Tests, was the poorest of his career – his average was 19.66 – and could be pinpointed as the start of his decline.

Gavaskar said at the time that his technique had suffered from his stint in county cricket during the previous English summer. No one, however, was convinced that this self-diagnosis was accurate. Even if his career was now on the downward slope, he still aggregated 500 against England the following winter and has, since that last Australian tour, scored seven more Test centuries. Gavaskar's record would have been even more impressive had he heeded the warning of his Australian experience and chosen to bat lower in the order. But he has always had pride and confidence in his craft. Moreover, India could not produce another opening batsman of sufficient class to replace him.

It was midway through the 1983 series against the West Indies before Gavaskar at last considered batting in the middle order. He informed the selectors of his preference, but said he would happily wait until they found themselves in a position to accommodate him. He got his wish in the final Test. He went in at number four, but gained little advantage from his new position as the innings was only 13 minutes and 14 balls old when he went in to confront Marshall and Roberts. It is now history that Gavaskar on this

occasion passed the Bradman record of 29 Test centuries and went
on to make 236 not out, his fourth double-century in Test cricket
and the highest score by an Indian against any country. This
innings was not as spectacular as the 121 he had made at Delhi
earlier in the series, but it was fluent and more typical of Gavaskar
for its solidity. Both must rank among his greatest innings.

Gavaskar's own choice as his most outstanding Test innings is
his 101 against England, at Old Trafford, in 1974. It is hard to
disagree with his preference, for England fielded a formidable
seam attack in that match and conditions were particularly amen-
able to swing and cut. Gavaskar overcame them with a truly
refined technique. Another innings of Gavaskar's that is quite
unforgettable, if for different reasons, is his 221 at The Oval, in
1979. Granted, batting conditions this time were ideal, and the
opposing attack on the day was less testing. But the circumstances
in which this innings was played were immensely daunting for it
began with India facing a deficit of 437 runs and more than eight
hours to bat for a draw. Gavaskar was supported by Chauhan in an
opening stand of 213 and India came tantalisingly close to winning. For sheer courage, concentration and stamina, this performance has seldom been equalled.

The lasting impression of Gavaskar will be of a patient player.
But he is versatile enough to have scored one of the quickest
centuries in Test cricket, against the West Indies, in Delhi in
1983. It came from 94 balls, with the first 50 having been plundered from just 37 deliveries. Indeed, it would be unfair to
remember him only for his marathon innings and his numerous
records, among which is the scoring of two separate centuries in a
Test match on three occasions. Unlike most great batsmen, he is
not an improviser. At the same time, there is not a shot in the book
that lies outside his range. If he cannot tear an attack to shreds, he
can certainly unsettle it with uncanny placement of the ball allied
to high skill in running between the wickets.

It was evident from the time that he first played Test cricket
that Gavaskar, born into a cricketing family, would one day
captain India and, indeed, he did. He led India in a record 40 Test
matches and won series against the West Indies, Australia, Pakistan and England. He has the distinction of being the only Indian
captain to win more Test matches than he lost. Yet his term ended

under a cloud. He was replaced after a tour of Pakistan during which India were heavily trounced in three successive Tests. Gavaskar had the background to become an outstanding captain. His batting record commanded respect and his skill, great esteem. He had experience, was extremely articulate and quick-witted. Tactically, he could most accurately be described as defensive. Strangely for an Indian, he had more faith in his seam bowlers than his spinners. But if his captaincy is to be put in perspective, it must be mentioned that he had at his command only two bowlers of true international class: Kapil Dev and Dilip Doshi.

There were never any obvious signs that the responsibilities of captaincy depressed his batting. But they certainly affected his personality. Gavaskar was always a man of moods and his moods became subject to more frequent and extreme fluctuations under his new mantle. The excitable side of his nature was never more apparent than during a Test in Melbourne, in 1981, which India eventually won to draw the rubber. For the only time in that series, Gavaskar had the measure of the bowling until, at 70, he was given out lbw to a ball which he believed he had very obviously played on to his leg. His anger reached such a pitch that he marched his partner, Chauhan, off the field with him, intending to concede the match, and it took the firm intervention of the team manager to prevent the Test from coming to such an unprecedented end, by default!

Controversy and jousts with cricket administration have been commonplace in Gavaskar's career. Most of his clashes with officialdom have concerned the rights and remuneration of players. Whether captain or not, he has been their main spokesman.

As for his own future beyond his playing days, cricketing success, a sound education and driving ambition have given him clear access to the world of commerce. He is on the board of a company that has a large share of the Indian synthetics market. He is also consultant to a soft drinks firm with involvement in cricket and he has an active interest in the manufacture of cricket boots. Commerce is by no means a side-line for Gavaskar. He takes it very seriously and works long hours at his desk between matches and tours. In a cricket-mad country, he is a personality commanding great influence, so much so that there could some day be a place for him in national politics.

The Authors

John Arlott

For over 30 years John Arlott's articulate, leisurely, confiding country-man's burr was synonymous with radio and cricket. John has now retired from broadcasting, but he writes as enthusiastically and as perceptively as ever from his home in the Channel Islands. He began work as a clerk in a mental hospital in Basingstoke and then joined the Hampshire Constabulary from which he resigned in 1945 on his appointment as a BBC staff producer. Faithful to the belief 'what does he know of cricket who only cricket knows', his interests are wide and varied. A collector of books, he wrote a lovely essay on the subject which was broadcast and has recently been published. He has written on wine, on which he is an expert, on cheese and on snuff, and on many other things in which there is an essential humanity. As a cricket correspondent he followed in the tradition of his friend Neville Cardus and wrote for the *Guardian*. A talented and generous man, he was awarded the OBE, but his greatest reward is the knowledge that he has given a love and understanding of the game he loves to millions of people.

Peter Baxter

Peter Baxter has become well known as the producer of *Test Match Special* and his work in this field, bringing together a diversity of talents, has won him the thanks of millions. So successful has been the programme and so great its following that Peter has now edited two books which tell, with typical good humour, of the work of the commentators and the making of the programme. His duties for the BBC tend to hamper his desire to watch cricket, but the broadcasting of Test matches has now become a vital part of the English summer, and winter, and for this, Peter Baxter is responsible.

Henry Blofeld

Henry Blofeld won a cricket blue at Cambridge in 1959, the year in which he scored 628 runs, including 138 against MCC at Lord's. He first kept wicket for Norfolk at the age of 16 and was considered one of the most exciting young cricketers in England. His first-class career was cut short

by an accident and he turned to writing and broadcasting. He has written
for the *Sunday Express*, *The Times*, the *Observer* and the *Guardian*, and he
has a wide following in Australia, where he contributes to many journals
and is a frequent broadcaster.

Michael Carey
A wide range of interests and talents has led Michael Carey from his
home in Derbyshire to all parts of the world. He worked as a freelance for
the *Observer*, the *Guardian*, the *Daily Telegraph* and *Wisden* before
becoming senior cricket correspondent of the *Daily Telegraph*. His honest views, forthright comment and economic style have won much
praise. He worked at one time for Yorkshire and Granada Television, but
more recently he has become known for his BBC commentaries both at
home and abroad, his north-midland view bringing a welcome balance to
the team of commentators.

Tony Cozier
The unrivalled authority on West Indies cricket, Tony Cozier founded
the *West Indies Cricket Annual* in 1970 and he has continued as editor of
that distinguished publication which has prospered in the years since. He
has covered all recent West Indian tours around the world and is a
renowned broadcaster. Among his books, *The West Indies: Fifty Years of
Test Cricket* is notable.

Matthew Engel
Matthew Engel hails from Northampton which, as he has remarked,
once threatened to be the sporting capital of England. He is now the
leading cricket correspondent of the *Guardian* and his witty and perceptive writing is in the great tradition of cricket and that newspaper. He has
produced some memorable phrases – he once remarked that he would
not believe Dennis Lillee had finished with cricket until he saw the stake
buried in his heart. Matthew Engel has made several tours with the
England party and is highly respected by those close to the game.

David Frith
David Frith played Sydney Grade Cricket to a high standard before
setting out on his career as a writer. He settled in England and edited *The
Cricketer* from 1972 to 1978. In 1979, he founded and edited *Wisden
Cricket Monthly*. He has several books to his credit, notably his biog-
raphies *My Dear Victorious Stod* and *The Archie Jackson Story*, and *The
Fast Men, The Slow Men, and England v Australia*, which was a huge
success. More recently he has set himself the task of unearthing film of

cricket. He has discovered some memorable pieces of great historic interest and the *Wisden* film evenings at The National Film Theatre which he organises and conducts have become great occasions.

Alan Gibson

An author and broadcaster of great distinction, Alan Gibson joined BBC West Region as producer and compere of radio programmes before becoming a freelance. He has contributed to several journals, most recently to *The Times* where his wit and scholarship, lightly worn, have won him innumerable friends. He has broadcast on cricket and rugby and among his books, *Jackson's Year* and *The Cricket Captains of England* have been very popular. A Yorkshireman who lived in Essex, he is now firmly entrenched in the West Country, a part of England for which he has a great affection.

Derek Hodgson

Derek Hodgson, having worked for several years on the staffs of national newspapers, became a freelance writer in 1983. He writes for the *Daily Telegraph* among other publications and covered the England tour of New Zealand for *The Times*. He edited a book on The World Cup which was published within two days of the final and he has worked on books with David Gower. He is particularly renowned for his knowledge of cricket in the north of England.

Frank Keating

Frank Keating chose to move from writing on international affairs to write on sport. His contributions to the *Guardian* and *Punch* have won great acclaim – in 1977 he was named 'Sportswriter of the Year' – and his honest, individual opinions are highly respected. He is still deeply attached to Gloucestershire, the place of his birth, but his writing has an international flavour and he is among the most popular of journalists.

Alan Lee

Alan Lee is a prolific writer on cricket and a knowledgeable and respected writer on the turf. He was a district and county schoolboy cricketer, but, when still young, decided to concentrate on sporting journalism. He has worked for the *Daily Express*, the *Daily Telegraph* and *Sunday Telegraph*, and most recently for the *Mail on Sunday*. He has written in conjunction with Bob Willis, Tony Greig, Rachel Heyhoe-Flint and David Gower and is noted for his charm and vitality.

David Lemmon
A former teacher, David Lemmon was the founder editor of *Pelham Cricket Year* which has now become *Benson and Hedges Cricket Year*, a most respected part of the cricket calendar. He has written a dozen books on the game including the first biographies of 'Tich' Freeman and J.W.H.T. Douglas. He is now working on a biography of Percy Chapman. Brought up on Compton and Edrich, he has lived in Essex for the past 21 years and has close ties with the county club. As well as writing and compiling statistics for *Benson and Hedges Cricket Year*, David Lemmon has edited the TCCB's official publication, *Cricket*. He is a collector of books, especially on cricket and his other passion, the theatre, and he is a regular speaker at cricket societies and dinners throughout the country.

Robin Marlar
Robin Marlar is the Honorary Secretary of the Cricket Writers' Club. He played for Sussex from 1951 to 1962 and captained them between 1955 and 1959. He was three years in the Cambridge side and captained them in his second year, 1952. His off-break bowling brought him nearly 1,000 wickets in his career. A man of many talents, he stood as parliamentary candidate at Bolsover in 1959 and since the end of his cricket career he has earned much respect as a journalist of forthright opinion. He wrote on cricket and rugby for the *Daily Telegraph* before joining the *Sunday Times* as cricket correspondent. He is the author of *The Story of Cricket* and a book on the England tour of Australia, 1982-83.

Christopher Martin-Jenkins
A keen cricketer who played for Surrey Second XI while at school, Christopher Martin-Jenkins scored 99 when leading Marlborough against Rugby at Lord's. They had been set 199 to win, but after his dismissal they lost their last 5 wickets for 12 runs and the match by 22 runs. *Wisden* failed to comment on the captain's heroic innings. He did not get a blue at university and was laughed at when he said that he wanted to write about cricket for a living, but a month later he became assistant editor of *The Cricketer*, the publication of which he is now the editor. He was the BBC cricket correspondent from 1973 to 1982 and still commentates regularly on the game. He is the author of several books on the game and an after-dinner speaker with a noted ability to impersonate his friends and colleagues.

Tony Pawson
Few men have given so much to sport and derived so much joy from it as
Tony Pawson. He began an exciting cricket career as a brilliant school-
boy and scored 237 for Winchester at Lord's. He served in Africa and
Italy in the Second World War and then went to Oxford where he was a
victorious captain of the university, which he also represented at soccer.
He played for Kent with great success and his soccer career continued
with Pegasus (where he gained amateur cup winners' medals), the British
Olympic team and Charlton Athletic. He was one of the last amateurs to
play First Division football. Since his retirement from those sports he has
become a fishing international. He has had a career in public relations
and has been a freelance writer for the *Observer* for many years. He was
Chairman of The Cricket Writers Club in 1979. A man of great warmth
and charm, Tony Pawson's writings have delighted people for nearly 30
years and it may come as a surprise to some that he chose as his hero a
'hard' man like Douglas Jardine.

Alan Ross
Alan Ross is a distinguished man of letters who was awarded the CBE for
his services to literature. He is editor of *London Magazine* and was cricket
correspondent of the *Observer* from 1954 to 1972. He played cricket and
squash rackets for Oxford and the Royal Navy during the war, but his
interests and his writing have not been confined to sport. He is the author
of several books, the most recent of which is his biography of Ranjit-
sinhji. A poet, essayist and independent thinker, Alan Ross is the only
writer here, apart from John Arlott, who contributed to the first collection of *Cricket Heroes*. His hero 25 years ago was another man of Sussex,
Hugh Bartlett.

D.J. 'Dicky' Rutnagur
A widely-travelled man who was cricket correspondent of *Hindustan
Times* between 1958 and 1966 and edited *Indian Cricket–Field Annual*
between 1956 and 1964, 'Dicky' Rutnagur has been a freelance cricket
reporter since 1966. He writes on cricket, squash and badminton for the
Daily Telegraph and regularly covers tours in India and West Indies.

Peter Smith
Peter Smith is the Chairman of the Cricket Writers Club. He has won
great praise for his warmth and diplomacy in handling controversial
issues and he has done much to foster good relationships between press
and players. He is cricket correspondent for the *Daily Mail* and was the

general editor and compiler of the official publication on England's tour of West Indies in 1980-81.

John Thicknesse
John Thicknesse relates his interest in cricket and his introduction to the game in his piece on Denis Compton. A man of wit and humour, John Thicknesse was on the staff of the *Daily Express* for two years before joining the *Daily Telegraph* in 1958. Three years after that he moved to the *Sunday Telegraph* where he remained until 1966. He became cricket correspondent of the *Evening Standard* in 1967 and has remained there ever since, noted for his good-humoured observation and pertinent comment.

Paul Weaver
Paul Weaver, who has won awards for his sporting journalism, worked with newspapers in Essex before joining the *News of the World* as leading cricket correspondent. He is noted for his forthright style and has conducted some highly-praised interviews.

Index